*Too many people on looking back see life, if not with
the bitterness of Shakespeare's Macbeth –
'a tale told by an idiot . . . signifying nothing' – at
least as no more than a chronological succession.
Claire Buckland in this book joins those whose lives,
with all their vicissitudes, are seen as an Odyssey,
following a course in which the phrase 'the art of living' becomes a reality. From such an interpretation
we can all gratefully continue to learn how to practise the same art.*

Phillip Hewett
Minister Emeritus,
The Unitarian Church
of Vancouver

*This is the odyssey of an indomitable woman, one
who has the clear-eyed courage to look both inward
and outward, and never hesitate to embark on a
new journey or to follow the dictates of a strong and
active conscience.*

Jim Wilson
Professor Emeritus,
Simon Fraser University

*Narratives from the Self unfolding over decades in
the stories of the elders must be heard and returned
to the community. As a woman of my mother's generation you modeled for me the integration of the
personal and the professional. You speak to all of us
who find ourselves 'always becoming' and needing to
know we are not alone.*

Margret Bridgford
PhD, Jungian Analyst and
Clinical Psychologist
New Mexico Society of
Jungian Analysts
Santa Fe, N.M.

Dream October 8, 1979 : Thanksgiving Day.
    I experience my life as the pages of a book, some tattered, some re-integrating into gray translucent sheets, but affirmed as a whole. What has been is an essential part, and the whole is Good...... Reflecting on the Beloved, I see the spine as a butterfly, and the butterfly as the heart... for healing and for transformation.

ALWAYS BECOMING

An Autobiography

CLARE M. BUCKLAND

Educator, Mentor and Jungian Analyst

PEANUT BUTTER
PUBLISHING

Vancouver, B.C.
Seattle, Washington
Portland, Oregon
Denver, Colorado

Canadian Cataloguing in Publication Data
Buckland, Clare M. (Clare Marie), 1914–
Always becoming: an autobiography

ISBN 0-89716-653-1
1. Buckland, Clare M. (Clare Marie), 1914–
2. Spiritual biography. I. Title.
BL73.B82A3 1996   291.4'092   C96-910500-2

Editing: Diana C. Douglas
Production: Fiona Raven
Cover Design: David Marty
Photo Credits: Don MacGregor, MPA, p.122
Jane Weitzel, back cover
First printing September 1996

PEANUT BUTTER PUBLISHING
Suite 230 - 1333 Johnston Street • Pier 32, Granville Island
• Vancouver, B.C. V6H 3R9 • 604-688-0320 •
226 2nd Avenue West • Seattle, WA 98119 • 206-281-5965
e mail: pnutpub@aol.com
Internet: http://www.pbpublishing.com

Printed in Canada

Author's Note: Quotations occasionally cite only the author and not the
source. I have been collecting insightful quotations all my life, and I regret
that it is now sometimes impossible to locate the exact volume from which
the quote is taken.

ACKNOWLEDGEMENTS

I wish to express my heartfelt appreciation to all those friends, in California, Seattle and Vancouver, who have encouraged me in the writing of my autobiography, and lent their support through diminishing vision and increasing fatigue, in particular to:

Anne de Vore, my Jungian colleague in Seattle, who said a few years ago, "You *must* write your story of recovering the Feminine." It took me a long time to begin, but her challenging remark remained with me.

The friends who read and critiqued the first draft in the early summer of 1995 — Jim Wilson, Sylvia Ommanney and my son, Frank Harris. Their comments and questions were immensely helpful.

My colleague, Ladson Hinton, who in spite of a very heavy schedule agreed to write the Foreword. I am deeply touched by his perceptive and appreciative statement.

The four friends who read the unedited version — Anne Ironside, Margret Bridgford, Phillip Hewett, and once again Jim Wilson — and have written affirmative statements which have warmed my heart.

Margaret Murdoch and Jennifer Getsinger, who have agreed to stand by for intensive proof-reading. They are themselves writers who will bring experience and skill to this demanding task.

Finally, to Peanut Butter Publishing and my editor, Diana Douglas, who believed in my project from the day we met. We have worked together joyfully, and her insight and perceptive questioning have made me examine more precisely what I *really* want to convey. I now understand why all writers invariably note the indispensable help of their editor.

Clare Buckland
Vancouver, B.C.
June 14, 1996

TABLE OF CONTENTS

Fate, nature and purpose are...one and the same.

My fate is what I am, and also

why I am

and

what happens to me.

Liz Greene

The right way to wholeness

is made up of fateful detours

and wrong turnings.

Free will is the ability to do gladly

that which I must do.

C.G. Jung

Man is the chooser.

He is not given freedom.

He has intentionality about freedom.

...only when he chooses to take the journey

to find the Self

will he *know* himself in the deepest sense.

Elizabeth Boyden Howes
and Sheila Moon

FOREWARD

By sharing the story of her life, Clare Buckland presents us with a generous gift. Her writing is a many-faceted jewel, each facet with its own individual sparkle of meaning, while the whole shines forth in a coherent unity.

She describes her story as a spiritual autobiography. However, it is not a "lofty" story about formal religion or conventional religious experiences, although those are present. Rather, her tale is about her lived spiritual quest. For her, human existence is in essence a quest and a spiritual journey. Clare has lived a life of passionate search and commitment, and has accomplished much in the world. It is her enthusiasm for life, for people, along with her basic vitality, which make this a "spiritual" book. This is the story of a life fully lived, leaving its unique imprint engraved upon the world, in contrast to the collective flow of time and history.

Her story begins in Vancouver and on a ranch in the rural Okanagan Valley. It is the story of an only child, a "father's daughter". The reader journeys with Clare through early family matters, education and significant mentors, loves and deep friendships, marriage and family, the evolution of career, into the ripening of age. The inner voice and perspective is never far away, and there is a constantly enriching interplay between her inner and outer worlds.

In her writing, we meet other deep souls who have nourished her, or whom she herself has nourished. A hunger for meaning, or perhaps a lucky fate, brought Clare together with many rich personalities in the fields of education, psychology, and religion. In experiencing these meetings, we join her in the fertile pageant of her eight decades. On another level, her story is also about our strange and turbulent century, with all its questioning and its search for meaning in psychology and religion.

Above all, this is the story of a life deeply and authentically lived, the tapestry of a life resolutely woven in strong colors. As I read, I feel gratitude to Clare for sharing her journey, her personal and vocational struggles, her growing maturity of awareness. It is renewing and invigorating to feel at first hand the powerful rhythm, the organic wholeness, of an actualized life. To live her story with her is to experience a renewal of faith and meaning.

Like Clare, we are all sometimes caught in the errors, blind places, the niches and ditches of our experiences. Often, faith in the wholeness of things is difficult to maintain. Through her long search, her "mistakes" and her sufferings, her discoveries and her transcendent moments, we feel, immediately and first-hand, the pattern which emerges. We deeply "know," through her story, the deeper rhizome of Being, of which we are the individual shoots. Clare has spent her eighty-plus years passionately embracing the moral challenge of being-in-the-world. As we accompany her in that process, her hard-won sense of meaning grounds us.

As a tale of a woman of this century, one who was a "father's daughter," some themes of her struggles for identity — such as the conflict between ambition and the "deep feminine" — will particularly speak to contemporary women. These perspectives may be especially meaningful for women who have not had a mother or other woman elder with whom they could share history and experiences.

However, it would be an error to call this a purely "feminist" writing. Her quest achieves that most deeply human level which transcends gender. The ebullient vitality of her personality, her depth of commitment, her integrity and authenticity, will delight and invigorate all readers. It is a search for meaning that defies any neat categories. She tells a profound tale of the human journey through life, with the individual coloring of time, place, and family.

Nearing the Millennium, Clare's story is a great gift, a summary of our times through the lens of the passionate and individual life of an extraordinary woman. The depth and length of the twentieth century speaks clearly through the fullness of her experiences. She invites us as companions on her Way. As we face the mystery of the future, her enthusiasm and integrity give us courage. The reward of reading this book is renewed faith and confidence in life. What more could one ask?!

Ladson Hinton, M.A., M.D.
President, North Pacific Institute
for Analytical Psychology

PREFACE

When the hero correctly names her own experience,
she aids others in doing the same, and thus supports
their journeys.

Carol Pearson and Katharine Pope[1]

This story chronicles the inner life of a woman who has lived
through eight decades of profound change. It is about Fate — the
cards we are dealt — and choice-making. It is about "wrong turnings" that lead toward wholeness. It is about spiritual development,
the continuing process of becoming who I really am.

Becoming one's own person is the work of a lifetime. The first half
of my life was lived in the shadow of a father who held center stage
while mother seemingly played a minor role in the wings. There was
no feminine model for success. That family pattern is typical of many
achieving women who grew up in the first half of this century, and
perhaps even more frequent among today's professional women at-
tempting to combine home and career. It is a pattern that has mani-
fold repercussions for work, for love, and for individuation —
repercussions that will be evident as the story unfolds.

I had to discover what a "feminine model" might be. In the 1930s
and '40s no one was talking about masculine and feminine principles
as two different energies operating in both men and women. Creativity and fulfillment, for both genders, involves both energies: being
and doing, relating and taking initiative. I didn't realize how lop-
sided my development had been as I focused on success in the
world. In terms of Jung's typology[2], I had over-used thinking and
ignored feeling and intuition, which in fact are naturally dominant
for me. One marker occurred at age forty when I made a decision to
be "Clare" rather than "Camie", which felt like "Daddy's little girl".
I had no awareness that I was wanting to connect with my underval-
ued mother for whom I had been named. My whole life has been involved with the recovery of the feminine qualities which honor
belonging and relationship, side by side with achievement.

---

[1]Carol Pearson and Katherine Pope: *The Female Hero in American and
British Literature*. New York, R.R. Bowker, 1981, p.256.

[2] For an excellent overview of Jungian typology, see Daryl Sharp:
Personality Types: Jung's Model of Typology. Toronto, Ontario, Inner City
Books.

I feel compelled to write this story. It is an expression of the ongoing journey toward a sense of my real Self. To acknowledge to friends that I am writing my autobiography at first elicited strange feelings of embarrassment. Who am I to think that anyone might want to read my story? Is this the mark of supreme narcissism? But the reluctance to say the word does not stop me. I need to stay with that inner necessity, and just write...even if only for myself. Mary Mason, writing about the autobiographies of women, quotes Mary Lucas Cavendish from as long ago as 1656, asking herself the question: "Why hath this lady writ her own life?" And since she felt that none cared who she was, answering her own question with: "...it is to the authoress, because I write it for my sake", and later adds: "I have made a World of my own." [3]

To decide was one thing; to begin to write was another. Like a stalled car needing a jump-start it took two friends to provide the impetus. John Geeza and Juliana, in Vancouver only briefly, had sparked long discussions of quantum physics and shamanic journeying, and one day suggested "a dialogue with a rock... Go and find a four-sided rock that summons your attention, frame your question, and we will guide the process." I found an interesting rock at Sunset Beach, and tentatively asked, "Is it important for my spiritual development to write my autobiography?" Asked to repeat the question three times, I heard myself say: "Is it important for me to write my spiritual autobiography?" I gasped: "That's different!" To write a record of the development of psyche? To write about my spiritual journey? Is my whole life a spiritual journey? The emphasis had shifted.

So I am sharing the story first with myself, and for myself. My perspective has come to be a spiritual one, and therefore perhaps has meaning for others also. Both purpose and chance are interwoven in the life of every living being, as the biologist Charles Birch has shown in his book *On Purpose*. [4] How I made choices and responded to unsought events shaped my journey.

Changes in my outer world have been equally profound. Change from a very British Vancouver, where I grew up, to a cosmopolitan

---

[3] Mary G. Mason in James Olney (Ed.): *Autobiography: Essays Theoretical and Critical*. Princeton, New Jersey, Princeton University Press, 1980, p.208.

[4] Charles Birch: *On Purpose*. Kensington NSW Australia, New South Wales University Press, Ltd., 1990.

metropolis. Change from an environment in family and school and church which was authoritarian, rational, black-and-white, toward today's focus on the need to honor difference, to embrace paradox and mystery, and to be a responsible citizen of the planet.

Living to please an idealized father and important others, as what has come to be known as a "father's daughter" is serious business! Even play is serious business. Stating feelings is uncomfortable. Oriented toward achievement from the very beginning, the balancing of masculine and feminine required conscious inner work. For me, this work involved many years of Jungian analysis and led to training to work as an analyst. Through it all has run the guiding thread of my religious commitment, enriched by seminars on The Records of the Life of Jesus. [5]

The degree of consciousness one brings both to values and to the challenges of chance is crucial. One's life, when seen from a spiritual perspective, embraces the realm of what is conscious, and also the vast realm of what is unconscious. To fail to pay attention to signals from the unconscious and instinctual realm — to hunches and anger and grief, and especially to dreams — leads to deviations from the chosen path. Yet those very deviations and dark places, those "wrong turnings" and "mistakes", come to be seen as gifts enabling a return to the path. Even physicists know that a chaotic element in their research may lead to a new discovery. I find affirmation in the work of Prigogine [6] in Chaos theory, that something gone awry, seen from this larger perspective, is an invitation to evolve toward a higher order of integration. This is Nature's way of evolving. Every difficult relationship and experience eventually enlarged my perspective and opened a new door.

Some ten years ago I examined twelve years of journalling and dreams and wrote about the woman glimpsed from that slice of life. Now I am challenged to look at the whole story, to discern themes, mark turning points, and perhaps catch holographic pictures from single images. The process is exciting. Bringing memories and images to life enlivens my sense of experiencing, of being more alive in the

---

[5] Seminars based on the original work of Dr. Henry Burton Sharman, and now presented from a Jungian perspective by The Guild for Psychological Studies, 2230 Divisadero Street, San Francisco, CA 94115.

[6] Ilya Prigogine and Isabelle Stengers: *Order out of Chaos: Man's New Dialogue with Nature.* New York, 1984.

moment. In the beautiful image of Clarissa Pinkola-Estés, it is to "collect the bones of lost valuables and sing them back to life."[7]

The importance of the process increases, I think, with age and retirement. There is a valuable book by Edmund Sherman, entitled *Reminiscence and the Self in Old Age*[8] in which he reports the affirmative results of research with groups of elders encouraged to reminisce. Even people in nursing homes, ill and discouraged, found a new sense of the meaning of their lives.

There is perhaps an even more mysterious need for remembering. I am haunted by Wordsworth's oft-quoted line: "Our birth is but a sleep and a forgetting..."[9] What have we forgotten? Our soul's origins? Our wish to become embodied for specific learning and spiritual development? I sometimes sense this Realm forgotten in the trauma of birth and the struggle to survive in a difficult world. Remembering becomes urgent in a process of re-discovering who I really am.

I hope what I write may stir your own remembering.

---

[7] Clarissa Pinkola-Estés: *Women Who Run With The Wolves*. New York, Balantine Books, 1992.

[8] Edmund Sherman: *Reminiscence and the Self in Old Age*. Springer, 1991.

[9] William Wordsworth: "Ode: Intimations of Immortality from Recollections of Early Childhood", Stanza 5, *The Norton Anthology of English Literature*, V. 2, Fourth Edition. New York, W.W. Norton & Company, 1962, p. 215.

IN THE BEGINNING

As I imagine my parents as young people there is a fairy tale quality about the couple: the handsome prince and the beautiful maiden. But in most fairy tales there lurks just out of sight a fateful quality, a problem to be solved. So it was with the two people who were to become my parents. My father was often referred to as "a Prince of a man", and my mother was the beautiful maiden — delicate, sensitive, and intelligent. They met in the years before the first World War in a western province of Canada, and had to wait for marriage until my mother-to-be had spent a year in a tuberculosis sanitarium in New York State. They married in 1912, bought one of the first Cadillac cars, and moved to Vancouver.

I was born a Capricorn on January 13, 1914, in a house on Laurier Avenue in Vancouver, and christened Clare Marie Metcalf Brown. Something must have gone very wrong at the birth, for my mother was ill with blood poisoning for some months. My father's older sister, Ada, was assigned to care for me. What bonding there may have been with her was destroyed as I grew older, for she was a sentimental woman, unfulfilled and a religious fundamentalist from whom I became totally alienated. No one ever talked to me about those first months, or about my preschool years when my father went off to World War One and mother was alone with her mother and sister.

Eva Clare Metcalf came from an old family in Pembroke, Ontario of British stock. I wish I knew more about them, for they were "different" with a strangeness that was never talked about. My mother was the only one of the four children to marry. One brother, Edgar, was sequestered in an institution in California, known to me only through his letters to Mother, written in indelible pencil, describing in detail his interest in horticulture. The other brother, Frank, lived in Vancouver, but we never saw him. Her sister, Belle, was a gifted artist, fiercely independent, who lived in a kind of voluntary poverty. When she died, she left the sum of six thousand dollars to my two pre-school sons — a handsome sum in the late 'forties. I still have some of her beautiful hand-painted china, and a watercolor of Halifax harbor. She was for me a *real* person, and delightfully non-conformist. She often brought buns from the day-old bakery, which disgusted my father and endeared her to me. Now my sense of the Metcalf family is of severe repression ...that perhaps the father, a judge, was harsh and judgmental, perhaps even abusive. I never knew him, and Mother never spoke of him. My grandmother Metcalf

My Mother
Eva Clare Metcalf

died in Vancouver when I was very little, unknown to the extended family or to me, since she had become addicted to morphine after surgery.

Frank Currie Brown was from New Brunswick, of United Empire Loyalist stock. His mother raised four children alone after her husband died, teaching school in Petitcodiac. Frank left school at thirteen to help support the family, and in the fashion of the Hero in search of adventure and to prove his mettle, pretended at seventeen to be old enough for the army and went off to Africa to fight in the

Boer[1] war. Education was important in the family — one older sister, Grace, was also a school teacher — and so my father became a great reader and thus completed "schooling".

The man I called *Daddy* was tall, stood very straight, and had a thick head of hair which turned silver white as he aged. I remember his hands as large, capable and beautifully shaped. His blue eyes often had a twinkle, and when he told a joke the punch line would sometimes get lost in his own laughter. He spoke with quiet authority, having no need to raise his voice for emphasis; in fact, I don't think I ever heard a loud voice or quarreling in my family. When irritated, Daddy just shook his head and repeated his firm opinion.

Most of my images of my father center in the house on Marguerite Street where I lived in my teens and college years. A typical scene in the evening after work, or on a Sunday, would find him in his favorite easy chair by the fireplace, pipe in hand, reading the newspaper or a book usually related to history and politics. He voted Conservative, and Churchill was a hero. Jews, Catholics, Americans, Asians and Europeans were "other" kinds of folk never encountered in our Anglo-Saxon world. Vancouver in those days was not yet oriented to the Pacific Rim, but turned back toward the British Isles.

My mother was educated at Ontario Ladies College, I think in secretarial science, but I'm not even sure of that. When I try to *see* her in my mind's eye I find it very difficult to discern details, such as the style of her hair. Apart from the look of anxiety around her eyes, which is always there when I recollect her, I have no sense of the expression of her face. She was about five foot five, and slender to the point of being thin, without any breast development. Once when we went shopping together for clothes, she bought a lovely green and black and white print dress with a pleated skirt, and the friendly saleslady suggested she wear some "falsies" — to which, to my surprise, my mother assented. She bought a necklace in the same colors — which I still have — and also some green jade earrings, and she wore that outfit with pleasure. I also remember her as they arrived home from a trip to California in a camel hair coat with a beaver collar, which complemented her brown hair and brown eyes.

That was my parents' first trip without me, and while they were away my favorite high school teacher, Miss MacDonald, stayed at the

---

[1]A war in which Great Britain fought against the Transvaal and Orange Free State, 1899 - 1902.

My Father, Frank Currie Brown

house with me. I enjoyed her stay so much that I'm afraid I didn't welcome them home very enthusiastically! On another such occasion, in my college years, I decided while they were gone to entertain some of my friends at dinner. Mother was really upset by this, and asked me why I had done such a thing. "Because you would have gone to so much work, and been so anxious about it, that it would have been a huge production." An answer she didn't appreciate, I'm sure....Years later, in Jungian analysis, I recovered visual memories of our home, beautiful with my mother's sense of artistry. I will write about that later, and about her garden.

In my early fifties I studied family systems, and spent a year in a seminar where people explored their family of origin; but only Auntie Grace was still alive, in her nineties, and she couldn't tell me anything about my mother's family. There might have been so many stories told, had I ever asked. I wonder about the difficulty children of my generation had in asking questions. Was it just the general repression in our family that inhibited sharing anything personal? Was it not proper to ask questions? By the time I was free enough to be curious and genuinely interested in *their* lives, it was too late. I feel sad about this. I remember giving a graduation address to high school girls in which I

"Auntie Grace"
Grace Brown Chalmers

urged them to get to know their parents as people...but no one gave me feedback. Perhaps when we are still at home we are too full of our own problems and interests to wonder who our parents really are inside.

The depth and damage of the silence only surfaced when I was about to be married to a man crippled from polio, and my father, fearing for my relationship, shared the dark secret of his own pain. He and mother, he told me, had never had intercourse after I was conceived. In my shock I could only stammer my sorrow, but could not invite him to talk about the suffering and repression this revealed. He added that he had been unfaithful to her only once. And later I put together some of the events of my sixth year: my mother had a heart attack and she and I spent six months in the east at a cousin's home where I can't remember seeing her at all; and there was a woman whose name my mother could not stand to hear. Whether the sexual act itself was the issue for her, or whether she was terrified of another pregnancy because she had nearly died in delivery, I never knew, because I couldn't ask *her*, either. The silence was complete except for my father's generous disclosure on my behalf.

As I try to reconstruct the family of my childhood, it has a nebulous quality. Speaking about it one day to a therapist friend, I found myself saying, "I only know that my father feels this tall" — gesturing with arms wide and high, indicating a giant — "and my mother is like a shadow over in that corner." She responded with, "I have an image of the sun and the moon...", and with an aha! sense I said, "A partial eclipse of the moon!". Wanting to discern the pattern, I began to search what journal records I still have in my possession: a high school collection of poetry, a few early pieces from 1949 when I was involved in Jungian analysis, and more extensive journal notes and dreams from 1969 to the present. Early memories are scant; I recall only a few significant conversations.

Without these written records as cues I would be at a loss to reconstruct the dynamics of our family. Alas! that I did not keep all my early ones. When I sold my home in 1972 to return to the University of California at Los Angeles for a post-doctoral year, I looked at the accumulation of journals and decided I *could not* cart them with me every time I moved, and I burned them. In the excitement of the new possibilities that lay ahead I didn't even register the sorrow of parting with these records of a troubled past. I was putting all that behind me — or so I felt.

Along with the lost memories of early childhood are lost photographs. They must have gone the way of all the precious items in my bedroom cupboard when my father, remarried, sold our home in Vancouver, and I was far away in Los Angeles. My father never thought to ask me if I wanted anything saved. Perhaps he felt I wasn't interested in my old home — another evidence of distance and unshared, even of unregistered feelings.

The early photographs are few, and most of them without context. There is one surviving picture of me on my mother's knee with the notation in my father's hand, dated 1970, the year before he died: "Dear Camie — taken before I went overseas, 1915 or early 1916. A really good picture of your mother. Dad." The sun is in our eyes; I am frowning, and my mother looking happy, eyes averted. There is one of me at three with my paternal grandmother, staring at the intrud-

Clare Marie at age 10

ing photographer. And one, a formal portrait of my father in full military uniform, gloves and all, and me on his knee, round-faced and satisfied to be on Daddy's knee. I must have been delighted to have him come home, but I have no memory of this. Another one, about the same time, finds me on the grass clutching a bunch of flowers and smiling naturally and happily.

First memories have to do with sex...a pre-school afternoon nap on the bed with my mother, under an eiderdown that followed me all the way to college. Like all children I had discovered the pleasures of touching a zone taboo to parents, and my mother stopped me. The other one is of comparing urination with a small boy, huddled in the back room of an apartment, using tin pie plates. I don't recall discovery.

I began school in the West End of Vancouver where we lived in a small apartment. My only memory is of breaking my glasses in reckless tag in the basement play area at noon, and being allowed to go home because I was dizzy from the bump on the head — and perhaps from fear. In that same era, my first effort to use a straw with a strawberry-flavored drink produced a shower of pink liquid all over my middy; it took quite a lot of practice to learn not to blow into the straw.

Somewhere in that year of becoming six a lot of difficult things happened. Our life experiences leave marks on us in many ways, even if we don't remember. These later showed up in hand analysis and my astrological chart, and perhaps that's why I was wearing glasses so early. I know (from being told) that my father was nearly electrocuted by faulty electric wiring in the office telephone; and my mother had a heart attack serious enough to send her east to Pembroke for prolonged bed rest in the home of a relative. I went with her, and went to school in snowy Ontario through that winter. The images center around tall, matriarchal figures in dark gray alpaca to the ankles, high black boots, high white collars, severe hair styles. No Mother anywhere in evidence — although I must certainly have had access to her. My caretakers were these childless women, most of them spinsters, no man in evidence.

"Camie" on father's knee, c.1915

Old houses. Dark wood. A nightmarish scene when one morning I was taken to someone else's house for the day, and decided in panic that I was NOT going to stay there. I fought off two or three of these figures in the front hall, kicking and screaming, until I undid the chain latch on the door and fled. The aftermath is forgotten; I hope someone took pity on that abandoned child.

Another scene, just after my sixth birthday, and in this same mansion where my mother rested out of sight, I relived in Jungian analysis, weeping...

> It is noon on the landing of the staircase, with the light falling on the window seat where I am putting Baby Ella, my Christmas doll, to bed. She has a china head, with pink cheeks and long brown lashes on the eyelids which will move to open and close her brown eyes, and brown curls like my own. I love her dearly, and talk with her as I tuck in blankets around her. There is a peremptory call to come to lunch. I delay, wanting to wrap her more securely. The call comes

again, "Clare Marie!" (the full name which meant "no non-sense"), and in my fear and haste Baby Ella falls off the seat and breaks. I am devastated.

I suppose she was the only available object or person to cuddle — what Jungians would call a Self-object. Her loss was still another abandonment, part of a long series which began at birth with my mother's illness. At two and a half I had scarlet fever and was hospitalized. And there were many leave-takings as my father went to Vernon, British Columbia, to train soldiers, and later overseas. He was sent home from Britain after severe typhoid fever which damaged his hearing. One of these partings I re-lived in a seminar training session in Zurich in 1987. Asked to stand "straight and tall" like my soldier father, I was then led to confront him in three-year-old style and tell him how I felt about his going away again. For the first time I experienced in memory the anger and tears that had lain dormant. Later, in elementary school, the longing to cuddle, to be hugged, became a conscious preoccupation as the search for mother substitutes began.

One other image surfaces from that period...a happy one of snow, and of tobogganing down a steep hill from the house toward the railroad tracks below. Someone must have provided a toboggan! Someone was active enough and young enough to play with me! I bless that unknown soul.

Much of my early life was spent at "the Ranch". A faded newspaper clipping found among my centenarian aunt's treasures (this is not the aunt who nursed me) contains the following paragraph about my father under the heading, "Pioneer Frank Brown Leaving Winfield".

> Of Loyalist stock, born and brought up on a farm in Petitcodiac, New Brunswick, Mr. Brown began his westward trek with a move to Calgary and later to the Okanagan Valley where he bought his first ten acres in Winfield in 1908; it was planted in 1909 and he built his home on the land in 1914-15.

The ranch was purchased under the terms of the Soldier Settlement Board, and consisted of ten acres of fruit trees — apples, pears, peaches, plums and a few cherries. My father named it Claremont, and it was dear to his heart. Later, he purchased an additional ten acres, and had a small herd of thoroughbred Jersey cows who were his pride and joy. One summer, when my college friend Mary McGeer (later, Mary Rupp) and I were at the ranch for a holiday, and my father had arranged to have a famous bull brought over for breeding, he refused to allow us to witness this event. That was not a "proper" experience for young girls.

The ranch house was beautiful in many ways, set as it was in a circle of maple and birch, and designed with much care. The fireplace was built of cobblestones gathered from the nearby countryside, and graced with an eight-foot mantle made of a split pine log still with its bark intact. French doors opened from both living-room and dining area onto a large screened porch where I slept and where I spent many happy hours reading. The bedrooms at the back of the house had open rafters in the ceiling, and I remember tales of a bush rat who used to collect small lingerie items and trail them across the rafters, to my mother's horror. The house was situated up a long hill from the main road, and faced the rolling pine-studded hills to the east, with Duck Lake visible nearby. When the afternoon sun cast long shadows across those hills the scene was utterly beautiful to my young eyes, especially as the sumac bushes turned brilliant red at first frost.

But during the war that must have been a lonely spot for a woman with a small child and her husband overseas...fifteen miles from the nearest town and three from the nearest village, without heat other than the fireplace, without electricity, and without a car. I don't know how much time she spent there during the war years; I only recall hearing her tell of a winter when the pipes froze and there was ice an inch thick all over the kitchen floor. Sometimes her sister was there with her, sometimes a woman friend.

My father used to speak of the marvellous black Lab dog who guarded me, but I don't remember him. After I was in school we spent every summer at the ranch. The trip before the rail line was put through to Winfield was an event in itself, involving the old sternwheeler on Lake Okanagan as far as Okanagan Landing, and then a horse-drawn wagon to our roadway between Vernon and Kelowna, marked by a gigantic pine. Eventually my father had a house built up the hill for the foreman and his family, and at one time their little girl Margaret was my playmate. Otherwise it was a solitary existence. A snapshot, now lost, showed me making mud cookies which I "baked" on shingles in the sun. Mother must have taught me to sew doll clothes while she made over old clothes to fit me. I rolled "cigarettes" from the cattail-like seeds of the birch tree; and puzzled over the appearance of our Airedale's penis as I waited down the road for the rural mail delivery.

In the 1920s annual chest X-rays were obligatory. When I was eleven the discovery of a small shadow on one lung banished me, along with my mother, to a four-month summer at the ranch. The doctor had recommended that I drink goats' milk, and my initiation was not a happy one because the neighbors' goats had been eating sagebrush, and the milk was bitter. But there were some happy "firsts" that summer. We must have had an old treadle sewing machine, for I sewed my first dresses for myself — and not the "Easy-Sew" variety, mind you! Those dresses, I recall, had pleats in the front, and set-in sleeves — one in a warm lavender color, and one pale green. I was proud of them. And that summer my father taught me to swim in the lake three miles distant. There was a road through from Kamloops to Vernon and on to Kelowna, and he must have driven up from Vancouver more frequently, and taken longer holidays. There were drives into Kelowna, fifteen miles south, to visit friends; and there was once a snapshot of me with my bicycle decorated for the competition in the village fair in Winfield. I picked fifty-three boxes of apples at five cents a box — my first earnings! — and learned to be at ease on a twelve-foot ladder. I remember skimming thick cream from the milk pans which were then stored in the screened cooler in the basement. That was the only cool place to be when the thermometer hit over one hundred degrees, and sometimes we would take folding chairs and sit down there in the hottest part of the days. I also recall hours of canning fruit with my mother, peeling pears, scalding peaches to remove the skins, pitting cherries. The kitchen would be steaming hot from the wood stove... I know all these things happened, but I have no memory of being with my father in the orchard, or of conversations with either parent.

Post-war unemployment had caught up with my father in the 1920s. It took him eight years to establish himself in a secure and responsible job. Was he depressed? Irritable? Were there arguments? I don't know. In 1924 a wealthy relative of my mother's in Pasadena, California, came to the rescue by offering my father a job with the Chamber of Commerce. I'm not sure how I know this, but I have a strong awareness of my father's humiliation. He was a proud Britisher who didn't like things American, and to depend once again on my mother's relatives — as when Mother had her heart attack — must not have sat well.

For six months we lived in that sunlit, palm-treed city, and some things seemed marvellous to me. In particular, it was sheer joy to visit my cousin's orange grove and gather windfalls into huge sacks, and eat all the oranges I wanted...sweeter than any I've had since! I loved the adult cousins, too — they were more easy-going than the Canadians I knew — and although their children were no longer at home I felt comfortable in their homes. School was another matter. In Grade Five we were studying the American Revolution — which I had already studied from the British viewpoint — and their "truth" and mine were in conflict. I was always in trouble for speaking out of turn, and arguing, and ended up once with adhesive tape over my mouth. Finally we returned to Vancouver and my father found work with the company he was to manage until retirement.

More images come to life from age eleven. We were living in an apartment across from Chalmers United Church. (The buildings are still there on Hemlock at Twelfth Avenue, although the church is now Anglican.) There was a gifted minister, the Reverend Mr. McGougan, who once a month provided a sermon for young people, illustrated as he went along with charcoal drawings on an easel, and I never missed one, although I'm not sure whether my parents attended church or not. I know they did not attend after we moved to the house in Kerrisdale. Perhaps because of the inspiring minister at Chalmers, I offered to teach Sunday School. But I was bored with the moralistic prepared materials and began telling my very young charges fairy tales from our set of the *Book of Knowledge* (an encyclopedia for young people), until I was caught and dismissed. My parents must have thought I was ready to join the church, because I came home from school one afternoon to find Mr. McGougan there, planning this event. I refused. Perhaps I already had a growing sense of independence and dislike of having something planned for me without discussion. Certainly I had not yet articulated a sense of religious belief that I was ready to affirm.

That same year I was passionately devoted to hopscotch, having a remarkable collection of "throws". These were home-made items to toss into the marked squares — bits of glass, strung beads, anything with enough weight to toss. One afternoon I got myself in trouble for not coming home after school early enough to greet my Auntie Grace who had arrived from Ottawa. This was a breach of family manners. I also breached their sense of decorum by doing handstands against the apartment wall, in full view of passersby...and we didn't wear jeans in those days! Christmas found me at the foot of my parents' bed unstuffing a long brown cotton stocking until I found a coconut in the toe — a rare treat in a poor family. I recall a box of clothing from the eastern relatives with a new wool dress for me, blue, with braid.

Then there is the first visual memory of my father. On a winter day in one of the heavy fogs we used to have, the car in which he was driving home from the Canada Western Cordage factory in Sapperton, near New Westminster, was struck by a train and dragged a hundred feet. Daddy was so severely injured that for a long time I was not allowed to see him in hospital, but eventually there was an afternoon on which he was first permitted to get out of bed and sit in a chair by the window. In my mind's eye I am standing nearby, and I watch him crumple with weakness, and dissolve in tears. I am feeling numb with confusion. I've never seen my father cry, and he is red-faced and embarrassed to have me see him this way. I don't think I even touched him, or comforted him. It feels like a long, terrible frozen moment. And then he asks me to call the nurse, and go home...I am appalled at this memory of physical distance, at my inability to respond, at the formality and code which must have governed our relationship.

Later that year my mother arranged to have my long curls cut, to emancipate me from the endless brushings and curlings into ringlets, and from my discomfort with being always the tallest girl in the class with these little-girl curls! I thank her for that, and for standing up for the necessity of this momentous deed when my father groaned at the loss. I must have been, even before puberty, what Jung would call his Anima Child.[2]

Grade Six was a difficult year. I remember being ostracized by my favorite friend and agonizing over this, trying desperately to find out what I had done to cause this — for I felt sure it was my fault. I remember, too, the tone of that classroom, presided over by a depressed middle-aged teacher who never laughed. One day she sent a friend of mine to the cloakroom for some misdemeanor, and at noon when the bell rang and Margaret emerged, crying, Miss Russell said: "Cheer up, Margaret!" Spontaneously I responded in a loud whisper: "Cheer up yourself, Miss Russell!" "Who said that?" "I did." "You will remain behind", and then she dismissed the class. I defended

---

[2] See Glossary.

myself by explaining that I felt Margaret had done her best and didn't deserve the punishment, but of course that was no excuse. I was sent home and told not to return until I apologized. When I went back after lunch, I said I was sorry I had been rude, but that I still felt the same way about Margaret! I think that was my first encounter with what seemed to me injustice. And also a first time going to the defense of someone who seemed to me an unhappy girl. Looking out for needy people became something of a pattern, the counterpart of which is the ego satisfaction of feeling needed.

At twelve the world changed. My father became manager of the Cordage company, at a good salary. He had a car of his own; and we bought a new house in a raw new suburb now called Kerrisdale. Marguerite Street has become treed and beautiful, and the house is still there at number 6081. In those days deliveries of bread and milk were via the lane in horse-drawn carts. Ice was kept in a box on the back porch. We had one of the first small radios, and listening to the Evening News became a ritual. Whether there were other programs, or music, I don't recall. The radio was in a small room at the back of the living-room, on the west side, and it was there that we had afternoon tea or coffee after dinner. The back garden was full of flowers — dahlias, gladiolas, roses, sunflowers — and my father planted a large vegetable patch. Later we had a Japanese gardener, Yamamoto, who came regularly to do the heavy work and cut the grass.

Two events from high school years come to mind. One of the eastern cousins, a minister's wife, came to visit us, and I adored her. She was very "religious" and a member of an organization called The World Christian Temperance Union. Because I adored her I took the pledge — only to feel some guilt later when I revoked the commitment. During her visit menstruation began, with much embarrassment. My mother produced some awful pads which had to be soaked and washed, which she actually took care of until Cousin Girlie told her about Kotex. That says something for my mother's lack of sophistication when it came to things sexual. And accounts for my own cluelessness when a school friend taunted me about not knowing what Kotex was, followed of course by my vehement assertion that I did know. I didn't know, and couldn't ask. That same year, waiting at the streetcar stop, I naively accepted a ride from a man who shortly afterward exposed himself. I opened the car door, and prepared to jump. He finally stopped, and I ran the rest of the way downtown to join a friend at the Saturday afternoon movie. I never told anyone about this experience. It wasn't until I was twenty-one that I read a book on sexuality, an idealized presentation of the mysteries of sex. This at least gave me *the facts* that I should have known in my teens.

Partly because of my mother's ill health and introverted disposition there was never much company at home, except for adult relatives. I came to hate Sundays with the inevitable afternoon drive around the park and the expectation that I would go along. Even the excitement of Christmas was muted by my assigned role of being polite and generous and entertaining. Not much room for rebellion in that household! Absolute, unquestioning obedience was the rule — one that my father later advocated for his grandsons.

A few years ago, reading *Personal Mythology*[3] by David Feinstein and Stanley Krippner, I found myself summarizing the internalized program of behaviors that I inherited in my parental home. From my mother: Do things nicely, properly. Create an attractive environment. Don't push yourself forward. Human beings deserve equal respect. From my father: Be successful. Be influential. Keep moving ahead in the world. Be informed. Keep to the middle of the road — no extremes. Be sensible. Hard work pays dividends. It was a world of decorum with an underlying sense of scarcity as a result of poverty, war and the Great Depression.

There was, however, one ritual that spoke of leisure and "enough". That was Afternoon Tea. I capitalize it, because it was an institution. My father copied it at his office; and later in my own home, even when harried by pre-schoolers and depressed, I never failed to stop what I was doing at four o'clock and sit down with a cup of tea. I still do!

When we moved to Kerrisdale in 1926 I was enrolled in a girls' private school. Somehow I had skipped three grades — three and five and eight. This must have been because learning in that day was largely by rote, involving memory and regurgitation. There was no such thing as an enrichment program for brighter children. Even art, as I remember, was stereotyped and imitative. We know now that skipping grades puts a child out of phase with her peers and in an introverted child increases the self-consciousness and loneliness.

[3]David Feinstein and Stanley Krippner: *Personal Mythology: The Psychology of Your Evolving Self*. Los Angeles, Jeremy Tarcher, Inc., 1988.

My parents must have realized that at twelve I would be lost in a large public high school. But I didn't have much respect for most of the teachers at this small school, and was bored by the lack of challenge, and often in mischief. The most fun was a summer afternoon when I took a skirtful of caterpillars into the classroom to plague a particularly inept teacher. At the end of that year I was transferred to a new independent school, St. Clare School, where I was to meet women who became lifelong friends, and who eventually invited me to become principal of their own school, York House.

Later memories cluster around college years in that same house, now rich in color inside and out. As my mother withdrew from people (except for her sister and one close friend) she poured her energy into the choosing of beautiful things for the home, and into her garden. I recall trips with my parents to antique shops for mahogany furniture for the dining-room, which was too small for the grand buffet with its carved grapevine curling across the back. They dreamed of someday "pushing the wall out"...a plan which was sabotaged, I suspect, by my mother's struggle with cancer, diagnosed when I was in high school. She plotted the rockery at the side of the house with utmost care and imagination so that there would be appropriate bloom, in the right spaces, month after month. Ironically, I enjoyed that rockery for the miniature bouquets it provided for a beloved mother-substitute, the Dean of Women at the university.

As I reflect on these memories I feel as if I had been a stranger in the midst of that family...as if the grain of the wood ran in a different direction for me, and there was no way to share my thoughts and feelings and elicit a response that connected. I felt tongue-tied, especially about my growing sense of a spiritual realm. Part of the problem of disconnection was situational, that I was an only child on both sides of the family, among many childless adults. To avoid unwanted kisses from these relatives I pretended I was undemonstrative. When I went away to boarding school at seventeen for a year and a half, I was never homesick; it was one of the happiest times of my life, having so many sisters! And there, too, I found another surrogate mother and relished her affection.

What sustained me in the years at home was a quality of introversion which made the hours alone in my room satisfying. It was a room with a dormer window where I had a large study table — a snug, safe harbor, with a variety of internal resources. I used to draw there, mostly copying small pen-and-ink pictures onto gift cards, or pencil sketches from a book on the chateaux of the Loire Valley. More creatively, I began having "quiet times" in the mornings — the beginnings of my own religious sense. Vividly, I recall one experience of intense light whose glow remains a permanent reminder of a further realm of consciousness. I also had good friends. One school friend with whom I have kept contact all these years was Marion Ross. She and I used to explore unfinished new houses after school...Marion small enough to crawl through the little doors where the milkman delivered milk in those days! Had we been caught, still in our school tunics, there would certainly have been trouble — but no one stopped us. Those explorations perhaps kindled my lasting interest in architecture.

I also received a great deal of positive feedback from my teachers. I was sturdy enough to stand up to them when there was an issue of unfairness — a quality my father labelled "stubbornness" — which has proved to have good survival value.

The notebook from those years is filled with poems cut from the newspaper or copied...sentimental, moralistic, nostalgic poems which belie the name. They belong to the *good* girl and echo her loneliness. Those that I wrote myself were full of yearning, evoked in the summers at the ranch, both by the lack of companionship and by the beauty of the Okanagan hills across the valley.

During doctoral studies at UCLA, in a behavioral science workshop, I created a symbolic representation of myself at age ten. I have a vivid memory of that afternoon class with Professor Art Shedlin. My ten-year-old was gray, a nun-like figure with drooping, covered head. When it came my turn to comment on my construction, and I identified with the overly serious, "uninteresting" ten-year-old, Art asked: "What are you going to do with her?" I promptly stomped on her. But the feelings lingered. My journal of that date records that "it was only when I deliberately moved back into the ten-year-old feeling that I saw my parents, my home, my total life, in pretty bleak terms."

I was fifty-five when I wrote that. Now, after the advent of the Women's Movement, sensitivity training, and much analytic work, I know that that was a jaundiced view, however real and poignant at the time. I'm sure that many women of my generation will have experienced a similar coloration of their childhood years.

My father's sister, the one who lived to be a hundred and was known to everyone as "Auntie Grace", once asked me: "Don't you wish you had given more time and love to your parents?" When I shook my head and answered, "No", she said sharply: "You should have. They both felt the sun rose and set on you." This cut to the quick. I couldn't find a response: She was right; and she was wrong. One part of me does wish that, profoundly. But the other part knows that no one of the three of us was capable of breaching the barriers. The inner core of me was not at home in that family, and the silence was powerful.

Just how powerful it was came home to me as I listened to Linda Gray Sexton reading a letter from her mother, Anne, the Pulitzer prize-winning poet who took her own life when Linda was twenty-one. A month after the suicide she rediscovered in her drawer a letter her mother had written her when she was sixteen...a letter full of affirmation and affection. And at forty, writing about her mother, she grieved in a new way. Listening, I was again in touch with the profound sadness that my mother and I had never found a way to share either our loneliness or our love. And like Linda Gray Sexton, I was only able to mourn my mother much later in life.

Today, I feel that sadness, and the unspoken appreciation. And the moon, my mother, is no longer eclipsed by the all-powerful sun, either in memory or in my inner life. Over the years the Feminine has at last found its rightful place.

There were many doors to be opened before that could happen. One of the first was boarding school — a whole new world of experience.

A WIDER WORLD

Memory doesn't keep a continuous landscape
but scattered patches of time.

Marc Hudson: *The Place of Memory*[1]

As I boarded the train for Branksome Hall, a girls' school in
Toronto, in January 1931, I entered a new world with a tremendous
sense of excitement. Having gone to university the previous fall a
very young, unsophisticated sixteen, and buried my head in studying, I had apparently grown so tense that my parents recognized the
need for a more congenial environment. This move was one of those
shape-changing markers for which I will always be thankful, the
first of many in the years of formal education beyond high
school...years that provided a series of leadership experiences that
are a major theme in my life; years when my relationship with my
mother and father became more defined, and when religion became
an orienting focus.

The train journeys back and forth to Toronto, winter and summer,
were themselves an event. I had my first expanding view of the Canadian landscape — the majestic Rockies and the endless prairie. It
took four days to make the trip, and every aspect was an adventure:
the Black porters making up the sleepers each night; the elegant service in the diner; the cinders accumulating grime in cars without air-

---

[1]Marc Hudson: "The Place of Memory" in *Journal for an Injured Son.*
Port Townsend, The Lockhart Press, 1991.

conditioning; standing on the open rear platform to enjoy some fresh air and the scenery. There were four of us from Vancouver attending Branksome, and we had good times together. I recall one very hot summer trip when the train was stalled somewhere on the Great Lakes, and with four hours to wait we headed for the nearest hotel, pooled our resources to rent a room, and took turns having a bath!

Ontario offered Senior Matriculation, the equivalent of first year university, and once again, because I was so young, the decision was made to take a year and a half to finish before returning to the University of British Columbia. I lived in French House, rooming with three others who had been at the school for some time, were older and more interested in boys than in school. I knew that two of them, who as seniors were permitted to go on the afternoon walk by themselves, used to meet boy friends en route. I certainly was not wise to the sexual overtones of some of the songs they sang. And while a uniform levels out some differences, when we dressed for dinner I felt not quite "hip". Moreover, the delicious starchy buns at recess and the more than adequate meals put thirty pounds on me in those eighteen months, and most of my clothes became too tight.

The teacher in charge of French House was Mlle. Helene Sandoz, who became yet another loved mentor and mother-substitute. She was a tall, spare Swiss woman in her forties, with a wonderful sense of humor and as ready as I was to share affection. After I graduated she came out to Vancouver to spend a vacation with my family. I have to be grateful to my parents, especially my mother, that they humored my attachments to teachers! I recall that while Helene was there, my father's close friend and business colleague, Major Anthes, was also visiting in Vancouver, and he and "Maddy", as my father called Helene, were attracted to each other. Nothing came of that flirtation, but later Helene met Karl Perry, and when they were about to marry, Helene asked me shyly if I could suggest something for her to read about sexuality. By that time I was more knowledgeable and could recommend Leslie Weatherhead's book on *The Mastery of Sex* (now out of print), an idealistic and beautiful description of intercourse. And in 1939, when I was married in Toronto, she and her husband, Karl, provided our wedding luncheon.

My greatest pleasure was music. I had an excellent piano teacher from the Toronto Conservatory, who started me off with two hours a day of finger exercises! I hate to think what it must have been like for listeners in the residence, but it certainly improved the quality of my playing, and I often played Debussy — *The Golliwogs' Cake Walk, The Flaxen-haired Maiden,* and *The Submerged Cathedral* — at the Sunday evening gatherings of the boarders. The greatest treat was being able to attend concerts at Massey Hall to hear great artists. One winter when I had a terrible cold the Headmistress wanted me to skip a concert engagement, but I pleaded so urgently that she let me go. The artist was Yehudi Menuhin, only fifteen, and I was in rapture. So was the audience. He played so many encores that finally he returned to the stage in his overcoat, accompanied by an older man, to signal an end. That experience cemented my passion for classical music, and I've followed Menuhin's long career with a special interest.

When I returned to school in the fall, after my first half-year, the headmistress, Edith Read, called me into her sitting room one morning to tell me that she had chosen me as the new Head Girl. I was so startled that I sat down suddenly on the arm of her chair and burst out with: "But I can't do that! I've only been here one term! There are others who have been here far longer..." She reassured me somehow, and told me to go and put on a clean middy (the sailor-like blouse we all wore) and be ready for the assembly at eleven o'clock. Alone in my room I tried to come to terms with this new challenge, and I remember kneeling at the window and praying for guidance in fulfilling my first experience with leadership. The duties were not arduous, involving chairing meetings of the Student Council — clan prefects and games captain — dealing with minor infractions of rules, and arranging special events such as the tennis tournament. That summer's tournament was a total failure. I, who was a poor tennis player, somehow reached the finals and was positioned against an equally poor player, who won. Disgusted, I talked to Mlle. Sandoz, who challenged me: "Are you just ashamed to have lost?" "No! It's a disgrace that the best player at Branksome is as bad as I am!" But overall, the students must have accepted me, for that year was the happiest I had ever had. When graduation arrived in June 1932, the joy of carrying the school flag at the head of the procession — led by bagpipes! — far outweighed the scholastic prizes I received. The gold medal inscribed with the school motto "Keep Well the Road", and the word "Leadership" is still a prized piece of jewelry.

Entering second year at U.B.C. I was a more confident girl, but still naive and with no idea of what I wanted to study or how I would want to work in the world. The most obvious thing to do was to pursue the subjects I liked, which were English literature and

French. I took another year of Latin because I had enjoyed translating Catullus' poetry, and in that year won the Latin scholarship, but I had no wish to continue. After one course in philosophy, which was mainly logic, I closed that door. And after one dreary course in experimental psychology, I closed that door also. When I became more interested in student activities I switched from Honors English to the regular program. I think my mind was unawakened, and in spite of some brilliant professors, nothing academic excited me. I was still shy about entering class discussions. And coming from girls' independent schools, and having had no brothers, I was still unready to relate to men. My friendships were with women, and belonging to a sorority enriched those contacts.

I continued to study music and practise two hours each day, working once more with a fine teacher, Mrs. Douglas Johnstone. However, in a student body of only twenty-five hundred I finally found the courage to run for President of the Women's Undergradute Society at the end of my third year, and decided that I would need to give up music. At the time, this didn't feel like a great loss, but in retrospect it was. I had been taught in a traditional manner to play some of the great classics, but not to sight-read or accompany; and the skill of playing the piano was quickly lost. The Steinway piano followed me everywhere I moved, unplayed, until finally around 1970 I sold it to someone who would make it sing once more.

The new position on Student Council offered real opportunity for leadership. I had become concerned about the situation of the majority of women students who did not belong to sororities and who for the most part seemed uninvolved in student activities and found it difficult to make friends. The Dean of Women, Mary Bollert, had heard of an organization called Phrateres, founded at the University of California at Los Angeles, which now had several chapters and was holding its convention in Seattle. Its stated purpose was "the development of the individual by introducing her to opportunities for leadership, unselfish service, participation in university... activities and a well-balanced social life."[2] Dean Bollert invited me to go with her to that conference to see whether this would be a useful or-

---

[2]Mary McGeer Rupp: "The Founding of Phrateres", in *The Way We Were: A Celebration of Our UBC Heritage*, Vancouver, Alumni UBC, 1987, p.43. I am indebted to Mary Rupp for this report on the fiftieth anniversary of the organization.

ganization for our own campus. We went down by Amtrak, were intrigued by the enthusiasm of Phrateres members, and decided to organize a chapter at U.B.C. in the fall.

One hot September day I called together the members of all the sororities — the Panhellenic Association — to tell them of the plan, and urge them to get involved. I didn't want the new organization to be known as a non-sorority alternative, which would polarize the women on campus. They agreed, and Phrateres was launched in January 1935 with two hundred and fifty members and seven subchapters. Mary McGeer Rupp was the first President. An editorial in the *Ubyssey*, the U.B.C. student paper, commented that while the effort to "bring about more contact among women students" was laudable, the support of all women would be needed or "it will have an ignominious death." Immediately, a cynical writer on the *Ubyssey* denounced it as "sour grapes", an organization for the "poor forgotten woman." I was furious. I encountered him at the foot of the cafeteria steps and shouted my rage (he was deaf) and tried to explain the opportunities for involvement and leadership for *everyone*. The next day the *Ubyssey* carried an apology from the journalist in a column headed "Mea Culpa". Mary Rupp reported in 1987 that "Phrateres has continued to flourish, a tribute to the idealism of its founders, its charter members, and those who have followed."

In retrospect, the motivation to launch such a project was a foretaste of situations that would capture my enthusiasm and energies many times. Some need in whatever community I was part of would become apparent, and provide an all-consuming focus for a period of time. Projects like Phrateres are a source of great satisfaction. Perhaps, too, they are part of the Capricorn's passion for building structures. They also are exhausting for an introvert and lead to a necessary retreat to rebuild and refocus.

This was what happened in that final year of university — not only because of the effort expended in organization, but because of tension in the relationship with my mother. Because of her withdrawal from the outside world, her denial of her latent capacities, and her fear of people, I developed a scorn for women who bury themselves at home, and was determined to have a professional life, to be as different from my mother as possible. The image of the frail woman with the anxious look in her eyes, whom I never touched or hugged, remained the dominant picture of my mother for years.

I had joined the Oxford Group Movement (a religious movement later re-named Moral Re-Armament) whose basic tenets were the Four Absolutes. One of these was Love. I knew I didn't "love" my mother. For me, this would include closeness and sharing, and both seemed impossible. The gulf became an agony as I tried desperately and without avail to develop that feeling for her. I would screw up my resolve to talk with her about our problem of distance, and could never manage to get words out. I tried to be loving and thoughtful, only to miss doing what she would have wanted. One unhappy example of that was my failure to obtain an invitation for her when, as Women's Undergrad President, I was asked to present flowers to the Governor General's wife at a formal University assembly. It had never occurred to me that she would want to attend, and she was hurt. One summer, on vacation at Qualicum Beach on Vancouver Island, I got as far as saying I was trying hard, only to hear her response, "You are not!"

I would talk with one of the Oxford Group counsellors, over and over again, but they were no help. For some reason, I never talked with the minister at St. Andrew's Wesley Church, Dr. Willard Brewing, whom I loved and admired. I suspect he would have had a broader perspective of the problem, and not been stuck with perfectionist absolutes. Nor could I talk with my father at that time, nor with the doctor who was trying to assess the cause of persistent wandering pains which no one could diagnose. At Christmas time in my final year, I was miserable enough that the doctor advised not writing the exams, and ordered complete rest in the holidays. In January, feeling better, I made a bargain with God: "If you want me to continue my leadership work, then please let me be free of pain." By some miracle of psychoneurological release, I was indeed pain-free until after graduation — and then the problem returned. I suspect that the thought of being at home with mother full-time during the long summer recess brought back the tension-induced body response. In those days even I could not have explained that there was simply nowhere to invest my intensity of feeling and my longing for the expression of love. Jung is cited as saying that "the more remote and unreal the mother, the greater the yearning and the more insatiable the need of the searching child."[3] I spent a full year resting,

---

[3]Cited in Patricia Fleming: "Persephone's Search for her Mother", *Psychological Perspectives*, v.15, #2, 1984, pp.127-147.

much of it in bed, reading philosophy and planning for graduate study.

A very different religious perspective had opened up for me right after graduation at the Student Christian Movement spring camp. There I encountered for the first time thinkers who were presenting issues of socialism, pacifism, and race relations. In particular, I remember Allan Hunter, a Congregational minister from Hollywood, a friend of Kagawa and Gandhi, whose church I later belonged to when married and living in Los Angeles.

I was swept off my conventional familial seat! And that began a new tension with my father, who by now held a position of national prominence in the business world as President of the Canadian Manufacturers' Association. His official photograph at this time shows a handsome man with a sweet pea in his buttonhole: it was characteristic of him to pick a flower en route to his car, and wear it to the office. This must have pleased my gardening mother. I was proud of this self-educated man who carried himself well and was loved and admired by everyone I knew, including my girl friends. I was proud of his success. But of course he could not tolerate my new-found enthusiasm for left-wing politics and we had heated arguments. It was as if I had gone over to the enemy camp, and I was as stoutly opinionated as only a new convert can be. I had seen the Light, and prejudice against Jews, Catholics, German salami and taxation reform belonged to a benighted past. Moreover, such attitudes were unchristian, so I felt, and I was taking the social gospel seriously. He was offended, and hit back at my naivety: "You don't know what you're talking about." I was angry and put off. The resulting sense of estrangement from the parent I loved added to the burden of alienation from my mother, and I felt very alone.

To his everlasting credit he supported me in my wish to do graduate work in the United States instead of Oxford or Cambridge, which would have been his choice. He even visited me in New York on one of his business trips when I was at Teachers College, Columbia, and we had a thoroughly good, non-argumentative time. He took me to an elegant restaurant on Fifth Avenue, and we shopped for gifts for my mother — gifts that didn't really please her. The watch we chose had a dial difficult to read; and the beautiful wine-colored silk kimono was a color she didn't like.

As I reflect on these years and the intensity of my religious and social feeling, I realize that I was imbued with the traditionally per-

fectionist stance of the prevailing Christianity. I read Thomas à
Kempis' *The Imitation of Christ* and wrestled with my inadequacies.
Two of my poems from that early notebook express both the sense of
failure to love, and my deep sense of connection with God. The first
was probably written at the Student Christian Movement camp, and
the second, one summer at the family ranch.

> *Father, forgive the cold love of the years,*
> *While here in the silence we bow,*
> *Perish our cowardice, perish our fears,*
> *Kindle us, kindle us now.*
> *Lord, we believe, we accept, we adore —*
> *Less than the best tho' we be,*
> *Fire of love burn in us, burn evermore,*
> *Until we burn out for Thee.*

And

> *In the early quiet of the morning I sought to be one with God.*
> *Nor sought in vain: for this my body is His temple.*
> *And I knew in that luminous moment of vision*
> *That Life was within,*
> *That there in my soul lay germinal*
> *A spark of the fire*
> *That flames in the skies of the newborn day,*
> *A breath of the spirit*
> *That scurries the clouds in their innocent play,*
> *And quiets the tempest.*
> *I knew and I know with unwavering faith*
> *That the thing that is I*
> *Is more than the driftwood afloat on the froth*
> *Of an unknown bay:*
> *I am my Soul,*
> *One with Life, with Beauty, with Spirit:*
> *I am my Soul,*
> *And my Soul is God.*

MARY BOLLERT

The most important figure in my university years was Mary Bollert, the Dean of Women. When I looked back forty years later, I realized that she was the first person from whom I experienced unconditional love. That is a rare gift in anyone's life, and happens perhaps only two or three times in an entire lifetime. She influenced my first choice of career; I did an internship in her office after gaining my Master's degree in Student Personnel Administration; and for decades my dreams pictured my longing for her after her death.

Mary Bollert was every inch a dean, the only woman at the university to hold that rank in a male bastion. She was one of five children from an eastern family where three of the women were professionals of stature in their fields. Florence was head of Sherbourne House in Toronto, and Grace was head of the Normal School in Vancouver. Dean Bollert had dignity. She belonged to the era of conventions. On the campus the large classes in English and Mathematics were segregated by sex; so, of course were the approved boarding houses. She is remembered by one woman student, Elizabeth Leslie Stubbs[1], as admonishing the freshman women "never to forget that as university women we were ladies, and therefore good manners, conservative dress — NO trousers, NO ankle socks — and propriety in all phases of behavior were important."

---

[1]Elizabeth Leslie Stubbs: "Dean Mary Bollert", in *The Way We Were: A Celebration of Our UBC Heritage*, Vancouver, UBC Alumni, 1987, p.21.

That included not smoking, and wearing hat and gloves to the rather formal teas for out-of-town students at Dean Bollert's home.

Perhaps because my own family upheld these same values, I was not put off by them, but responded, instead, to her warmth. When as a sixteen-year-old in my freshman year I was burying myself in studies, lonely and stressed, it was to Mary Bollert I talked about dropping out at Christmas and postponing my scholarship. And that first meeting established a connection at a heart level: she *understood*, and kissed me good-bye.

A year and a half later, she and her sister Florence attended the graduation ceremonies at Branksome Hall, and Mary invited me to tea with them at Sherbourne House. That was more important to me than that my father was also at my graduation! In the three years at U.B.C. I visited with her often, and it was she who checked the graduation lists to see whether the names were simply alphabetical with "Brown" at the top of the list; or whether, indeed, I had graduated at the head of the Arts faculty (not including Honors students). I don't know who was more pleased that I had, indeed, come first. We shared discussions about the Oxford Group Movement, and to her I poured out my difficulties with mother.

After graduation, when the psychosomatic pains returned, my parents arranged for me to spend a week at a therapeutic center in Victoria, and Mary Bollert came over to join me on the weekend. She had a heart condition and was weary at the end of the academic year. I was in bed when I heard her arrive at the room next door, and after a little while I knocked. She was already in bed for a rest, and threw open the covers to invite me in, and held me close. Mary was my mother's age, and I was twenty — but for the first time in my life I was a child in the arms of a "mother" who was able to express her caring, where there was no blocking. It may be that when I was tiny, my own mother had been able to do that, but not within my memory. To be welcomed in that fashion still feels like a miracle, as I recall the sheer joy of that moment.

The decision to train to become a Dean of Women was made with Mary, whom in those days I addressed as "Miss Bollert". I had learned that there was a special course of studies at Teachers College, Columbia University, called Student Personnel Administration, designed specifically for deans of men and women. My father agreed to finance these studies, and off I went to New York in 1936. I wrote

Mary Bollert

Mary often about my excitement in the program, and the extraordinary experience of New York itself.

To a young woman from a conventional British-type background, and the youngest in the class, the city was overwhelming. I wrote an impassioned poem about "New York: City of Contrasts", for indeed the gulf between the extreme wealth evident on Fifth Avenue and the poverty of Harlem was appalling. In the 1930s it was still possible for a white woman to walk in Harlem. The only forbidden area, indicated by warning signs in the residence, was Morningside Park where even then assault and rape were a danger.

New experiences abounded. I went to the Metropolitan Opera for the Ring Cycle, sitting in "the gods" with other students for a one dollar ticket! A Black preacher, Father Divine, was the toast of Harlem in those days, and I joined a Fellowship of Reconciliation tour to Father Divine's "Heaven" where on the upper floor of an old building chicken dinners were dispensed, and the singing and stomping shook the floor we stood on. I was struck by the fact that the only people who went into trance were a few white women standing against the wall. The black people were simply exuberantly happy.

Other experiences stand out. A friend and I went on a double date one night to a club where the strip artist was so beautiful that I was spellbound. The men were apologetic: "We shouldn't have taken you there!" But I loved it... My closest friend was a woman from Greenwich, Connecticut, who sometimes invited me to go home with her for a weekend. One evening we went to a movie, and I was horrified that people booed the picture of Franklin Roosevelt when his image came on screen. For me, he was a great man... Another student in the class was a fundamentalist, who also invited me and another woman for a weekend in her home, and clearly wanted to convert us. She was even trying to convert a Jewish friend. That, too, was unthinkable in my book.

The most valuable religious experience was attendance at Riverside Church where Harry Emerson Fosdick preached each Sunday. There was a membership of thirty-five hundred, and I had to have a Student Membership card to get in. I hardly missed a Sunday, and I attended his evening series on Miracles, appreciating the liberal approach which I had first encountered with Dr. Brewing.

In spite of all these new adventures, the old habits of intensity and perfectionist study were still a part of my being, and once again my body reacted with the wandering pains. This time, my senior professor referred me to a wise woman physician who asked probing questions about my social life — and was I dating? — and saw clearly that tension was the source. She sent me to a woman who described herself as a "structural hygienist"; and there I learned to breathe! and to do stretching exercises. No more pain. Even today, I still have to be reminded to "Breathe!" and without morning yoga-like stretching I would be more tired and stiff than I am.

Once again, I remember little of the content of the classes, which focused largely on the practical isssues of counselling students and dealing with problems of failure, prejudice, economic straits and vocational guidance. Discrimination against women and sexual harassment had not yet surfaced, but were no doubt happening. What I recall most vividly is the personalities of the two major professors, Sarah Sturtevant and Esther Lloyd-Jones, who made a deep impression on me. They were more than "academic"; they were women of the world, alert to social issues and cultural influences impacting on students. When I stayed on for Summer Session in order to complete my degree in one year, I encountered another thoughtful professor who taught educational philosophy and I was introduced to John Dewey and Horace Mann. One concept that impacted me strongly was the current theory of *abundance* in contrast to scarcity: the notion that there is *enough* to meet people's needs. Coming out of the Great Depression, and raised in a household that stressed frugality, this was for me a liberating idea. Now, of course, we know that natural resources are not endless and that we must conserve. It will require major shifts in values and organization for there to be enough for everyone.

In one of those summer classes I met John Meador, a young teacher of my own age. He invited me to go one night to Coney Island, and we took most of the rides, including the highest loop-the-loop. John said he hoped I wouldn't be too scared; the last time he had taken that ride with a woman, she had torn his shirt, clutching him so hard! The ride took my breath away, but I loved it. And John and I became correspondents after I returned to Vancouver. Clearly, we cared a lot about each other. But the relationship foundered when I suddenly decided to enter the ministry. This decision was short-lived, and certainly the result of the "specialness" of a girl giddy with success and praise who was going to "give herself" in some magnificent gesture to the Church. When his letters ceased to come, I was very sad; but when I came down to earth John and I resumed correspondence. A year later, planning to do summer study at Pendle Hill, a Quaker graduate study center in Pennsylvania, I wrote and asked if he would be willing to meet me at the train station in New York. He did, and later he drove out to Pendle Hill one Sunday to spend the afternoon with me. It was a completely happy time.

Alas! Fate, she whom the Greeks named Moira, intervened. It is she who does the bidding of the Self when the soul's choice of destiny lies another way.[2] By the time John came for that visit, I had fallen in love with Morgan Harris, caught in the net of a man of wider experience who had been studying there all that year. He saw what was happening with John, and promptly asked me to marry him. Spontaneously and without any thought, I agreed. Years later, distraught with depression and unhappiness, I tried to reach John, but of course the letter was returned, "unknown at this address". I became even more hopeless, but there is no turning back from a path, however unconsciously chosen, if that way lies destiny.

That marriage is a story in itself, but I want now to return to tracking the relationship with Mary Bollert, leap-frogging over decades in which her influence colored my life. There have been many remarkable mentors, but none who so captured my unmothered self and commanded my devotion.

The summer after my return from New York, Mary came for a visit at the ranch where mother and I were spending the summer. I'm sure it was not easy for my mother to extend this courtesy to a woman who was a rival for my attention and caring, but her innate courtesy prevailed, and the days seemed without tension. Mary and I had few times alone, except when I took her for a long drive up into the Okanagan hills; other trips were shared.

In the fall I began my internship in Dean Bollert's office, thanks to Mary's arrangement with President Klinck for official status and a small stipend. That was a wonderful year for me, but not always without strain for my mentor. I was young and full of ideas from my studies in Student Personnel Administration, and I think Mary felt challenged. One project in particular implied a need for more supportive contact with women students in their first year. I persuaded her to send a letter to the students who had not done well in the Christmas examinations inviting them to come in for a talk — which I suspect produced more anxiety than reassurance of assistance. I don't really know whether any of those students found it easier in future to come to the Dean's office for consultation.

At the end of that year President Klinck asked to see me, and we discussed the possibility of my succeeding Dean Bollert when she retired, which might have been soon because of her health. He had been impressed by an article I had written for the Student Christian Movement journal in which I had offered the comment that in addi-

---

[2]I write about Fate in Chapter Four.

tion to an academic environment promoting individual development, we needed a perspective that included the religious dimension. He felt I needed a year on another campus to enlarge my
experience. I was only twenty-four, and I probably needed several!
But we agreed that I would accept an invitation to be Student Christian Movement co-secretary at the University of Toronto. While
there, I served as Don for one of the graduate women's residences.
The year was not a very happy one for me, partly because I was
working with a very theological colleague who expected knowledgeable discussions of current philosophical issues, and my orientation
was to students' personal lives and dilemmas and their spiritual *experience.*

Also, by that time I had become engaged to Morgan Harris, who
was in New York, and I was preoccupied with an active correspondence. At the end of the year President Klinck came to see me in my
office, and when I told him about Morgan, he stated flatly, "Well, in
that case, I think it unsuitable for a married woman to hold the position of Dean of Women." This was 1939. Some years later, married
and living in California, I applied for the same position at Occidental
College, and was told: "My dear, you are going to want to have children, and this is no profession for a family woman." That's the way it
was in those days. I just accepted it. Today I am appalled. Times have
changed, thanks to the Women's Movement. The fact remains that I
was not psychologically ready for either of those positions. Nor was
that my destiny.

In 1944 I went home to Vancouver with my first son, Reed, who
was then about nine months old. I wanted Mary to see him when he
woke from his morning nap, so she came to the house, walking
slowly up the steps. All I could say was "Mary!" as I flung my arms
around her; and she returned the hug, exclaiming with the same delight, "Clare!" It seemed a long time since I had experienced that
kind of mutual joy. When Reed announced his waking by shaking
the crib upstairs, we climbed the stairs slowly together, careful for
her heart, and opened the door. There was Reed, standing and beam-
ing at us both, and I introduced Mary with the words: "Reed, this is
someone very dear." He seemed to know, and smiled at her. She enjoyed the ritual of the morning bath, watching from a chair. Happiness hung in the air. My mother had not lived to see her grandsons,
and Mary's appreciation was golden.

When my second son, Frank, was a baby, Mary's heart stopped beating one day, and I received a telegram from my father informing me of her death. I vividly remember crying into the sink as I washed dishes, and saying, to myself if not to Morgan: "There will never be enough love." Those were desolate years, and even though Mary and I had seldom seen each other, or even written many letters, for me it had been important that she be in the world, this woman who understood me, and loved me unconditionally.

I had already begun a long period of Jungian analysis, first with Hilde Kirsch, and later with Max Zeller. Journals from those years are lost, but there were constant dreams of trying to reach Mary; or of her dying; or of trying to help her die. Max interpreted these as a need on my part to let go of an older style of conventional living; and I never managed to convey to him how important she had been in my life. Perhaps I didn't realize it at the time; or perhaps I hadn't the self-confidence to make deep feelings known. Indeed, I did need to let go of the perfectionism that dominated my life, but the real Mary had to be mourned before the dream Mary could die. It was not until I resumed Jungian analysis in 1979 as I entered training, that analyst John Allan saw the full significance of this mother figure, and helped me both appreciate that and mourn her loss. In addition, that had to be done before I could resolve the alienation from my own mother. I stopped dreaming about Mary, except for occasional joyful contact, until I left for a seminar in Zurich in 1987. There, I had to come to terms with the conventional woman inside me, who like the Old Queen of fairy tales had become stuck in an outworn pattern.

I had signed up for that six-week seminar on impulse, inspired by the report of a close friend, and somehow sensing a need for "breaking out", or "breaking through" into a new experience of life. At seventy-three I was definitely feeling "older" and not yet experiencing aging as a process of becoming free — free of the compulsion to do "the right thing", free of caring about deficiencies. I wanted to live *that* way. I described the urge, in my journal, as wanting to be "up-ended". I did just that, in unexpected ways.

My journal of January 17 records a dream from a short sleep on the plane to London.

> *I am in a group where Mary Bollert is present. It is time to leave. I start out the door with the people I am driving with, and say, "Just a minute..." because I want to say*

good-bye to Mary, who is standing there in the hallway. We go back into the room together. I take both her hands, and look at her, deeply. She shrinks in size to a small, wizened woman, and says, "I am very old. People do not realize I am ninety." She seems ready to die. I feel great, overwhelming love, and as she speaks I am waiting to say, "Mary, I love you more than anyone else in the world." I waken.

As I write, I feel the love and the tears. It is as if she is linked to my soul — even as when I was a young woman. I haven't dreamed of her for so long...Is she the "older" part of me that is ready to die? the "older" mind-set? I want to embrace her before we part — to affirm *that* side of me that is related to the Father/Mother archetypes.[3]

A month later I literally enacted the "upending" by slipping on the ice and injuring my right hip. In a dream a few days later a voice says: *"Observe carefully who needs to be upended."* I look, and see a stick figure of the Queen. It happens in a twinkling. I understand the meaning... But it took me five days to get up courage to deal with the pain and the dream in a work session. That evening I volunteered to work in the center, and limped forward. The leader asked what my problem was, and I said: "I upended myself on the ice." "And who got up-ended?" "The Old Queen", said I, spontaneously, surprising myself.

What I came to understand that evening was that the conventional queen had been over-turned: the proper, dignified father's daughter. In my journal I listed the qualities associated with that part of me: reserved, quiet, serious, careful, cautious, "nice", doesn't ask for help, can be counted upon to be always the same. How boring! What I at last *wanted* was to speak my mind, to be angry, to call on friends for help when I need them, to be in tune with my damaged instinctual side, my body. I wanted to be in authority in my own life. Alive!

One of the wonderful experiences of that seminar happened during that time of pain. Three women in the residence worked with me as I lay on the bed, bringing to life the qualities of the black panther, an animal who attracts me. It felt as if the command, *Be Careful*, had got locked in the constricted hip. A panther can "sniff out" danger without being *too* careful. I moved, and growled! and the three

---

[3]See Glossary.

women became big Cats with me. Judith spoke of there being "too much gentleness; of the need to be sharper with insights, not sparing, respectful of the Great Cat, in tune with its power." This was the kind of highly charged fantasy that was missing in my childhood, overlaid with rationality.

It was not until the end of the six-week seminar that I recalled the dream on the plane in which I had bade Mary a loving good-bye because she herself was "very old" and ready to die. She would understand the need for my transformation, as she always had. And so it is that the gift of her unconditional love remains as a blessing.

Recently, in a seminar on alchemy I once again faced the imagery of the Old King and Queen needing to be dissolved and transformed and reborn as living principles. The theme occurs over and over again in fairy tales, where a land in disarray is suffering because the *old* king (or queen), often without a consort, needs to die. This is a challenge in middle age, and even more so in old age. I will write about that in a later chapter.

Now, I need to turn back the clock to the time of my marriage to Morgan Harris.

4 FATE: IT HAS BEEN WRITTEN

Fate, nature and purpose are ... one and the
same. My fate is what I am, and what I am is also
why I am and what happens to me.

Liz Greene

Free will is the ability to do gladly that which I
must do.

C.G. Jung

The fate that brought Morgan Harris and me together was certainly less romantic than the seemingly auspicious union of my parents. Shadows loomed from the beginning, but I was unaware and confident all would be well. The road to being able to say "I would not have had it otherwise" has been long and difficult. I am finding that writing about this period of my life arouses sadness, even though the fruits have been many.

In the course of Jungian analysis I encountered the work of Liz Greene, herself an analyst, and read her profound book, *The Astrology of Fate*. From her I gained new perspective on the meaning of the darkness I encountered in that marriage — darkness which I walked into blindly. Greene reports that from what she has observed in her analytical and astrological work with clients,

> "there is certainly something — whether one calls it
> fate, Providence, natural law, karma or the unconscious
> — that retaliates when its boundaries are transgressed or
> when it receives no respect or effort at relationship, and
> which seems to possess a kind of 'absolute knowledge' not

only of what the individual needs, but of what he is going to need for his unfolding in life." (p.8)[1]

Later she writes about the need to *trust* fate, and goes on to speak of the values of depression in learning to respect the disintegration of old identity:

> ...how can one trust it, unless one has spent time in despair, darkness, rage and powerlessness, and has found what supports life when the ego can no longer make its accustomed choices? (p.37)
>
> How can I believe hopefully in something which I cannot see and do not understand? What have I done to earn such a fate: where does my fault lie? What if the blank emptiness simply goes on and on? Any experience of deep depression carries with it the firm sense that nothing will ever change. It might therefore be appropriate...for us to recognize also the mark of an initiation into the irrevocable, and a need for genuine reverencing of depression and despair. (p.38)

Who was Morgan Harris? He was born in Colorado in 1905, and had suffered damage from polio at age five. For years he had worn braces, but had fought valiantly to compensate for the loss of running like other kids by learning from books how to coach tennis. Later he sailed and paddled a canoe. He had gone to spend a year of study at Pendle Hill. In Pennsylvania he had worked also with physiotherapists who enabled him to reactivate unused muscles, and he had been able to abandon the braces and use two ski poles, and later just a cane. Such a transformation takes courage.

We met at Pendle Hill in the summer of 1937. I had gone there to spend a month studying with Gerald Heard, a brilliant Irish scholar and philosopher who had been Science Editor for the B.B.C. in England. His subject was "An Inquiry into the Origin and Growth of the Sense of Spirit". I found his lectures spell-binding. I had gone to that program in preparation for my work as Student Christian Movement Secretary at the University of Toronto. Fate had a hand in this move also, for my first choice had been to go to Lake Minnesing

---

[1]Liz Greene: *The Astrology of Fate.*York Beach, Maine, Samuel Weiser, Inc., 1984.

in northern Ontario to study the Records of the Life of Jesus with Dr. Henry Burton Sharman. That choice had been side-tracked because the man who was to be my co-secretary, Dr. Wilfred Lockhart, was antagonistic to that study. In fact, he proved to be so ultra-conservative theologically that I felt he should have been an Anglo-Catholic, and we had great difficulty working together.

In contrast, Morgan and I canoed and swam and discussed ideas endlessly. The Quaker approach to religion appealed to me instantly: to be guided by "the inner light" instead of a creed felt utterly liberating, and we shared this response. Morgan seemed to me to belong to the wider world that had beckoned at that Student Christian Movement camp, and I was captivated. He had a wonderful smile, warm and engaging, although it was not easy for him to be in touch with feelings. I remember being puzzled later by his tendency to "tear" when touched by something; it was a struggle to allow his heart to speak. But he *knew* what he believed, to the point of being opinionated — like my father! The difference was that he was an intellectual and committed to his view of the world and to social movements. That appealed to me.

We quite literally "fell" in love, and became engaged before the month was out. Afterward, we both attended the World Youth Congress in Poughkeepsie, New York, where I shook hands with Eleanor Roosevelt, deeply impressed by her dignity and humanity — and then drove on north toward Toronto.

I recall vividly rowing on a lake near Albany surrounded by hills ablaze with autumn color reflected in the still water. But most of all I remember my trepidation at registering at a motel as "Mr. and Mrs. Harris" and our first night of love-making — *my* first sexual experience, which resulted in bloody sheets from the breaking of the hymen. And my anxiety about pregnancy until my next menstrual period. This was 1938, before sexual freedom and sophisticated birth control. When Morgan visited Toronto the following spring, I refused to take the risk and once again endure that anxiety.

In Kingston we stayed with my mother's cousins, Girlie and Will Brown. Two things happened that should have alerted me to trouble ahead. One afternoon as I was resting in the guest room, Cousin Girlie came in with tears in her eyes, and tried to tell me that she was afraid for me in this relationship. I'm sure, now, she was troubled by Morgan's crippling from polio; but more than that, she must have seen clearly the great gulf between our backgrounds. I'm sure, too,

Clare Brown & Morgan Harris
September 23, 1939 at their wedding

that Morgan was equally uncomfortable in their conventional religious home, and to my great embarrassment he did not thank them
for their hospitality as we left. I wasn't in accord with their conser-
vatism either, but I loved them and felt the discourtesy and the tension. In love, and too unconscious to realize the significance of this
small sign, I said nothing.

We decided to marry the following September, 1939, and I wanted
to accept a summer job at the camp where Morgan was to be working. A telegram from my father put a stop to that: "You must spend
the summer at home. Your mother is ill and needs you here."
Stunned, I agreed. Her cancer had returned, and was inoperable,
and this would be my last opportunity to spend a period of time at
home with her. She made a great effort to accept my engagement,
and shopped with me, and even gave a tea inviting all the family
friends. This must have been extraordinarily difficult for both my
parents, feeling as they did that the marriage was unsuitable and
fraught with future trouble: Morgan was an American, crippled, and

I hadn't known him very long or met his family. I was defensive, unwilling to discuss the matter.

So the marriage proceeded, in the Quaker Meeting House in Toronto, my father refusing to attend. My mother wasn't well enough to travel. My old friend, Helene Sandoz, now married, gave the wedding luncheon and Major Anthes, my father's friend, attended out of courtesy. Morgan and I packed his car with the wedding gifts and drove to New York via Niagara Falls. I remember the Customs officer asking what we had to declare, and I mentioned the silverware having a certain value. "And is that all you wish to declare?" Yes, I answered truthfully! Perhaps he knowingly asked the question in that form, recognizing us as newlyweds. In any case, we could have cleared it all as "household goods", but it was kind of him not to require us to do all the paperwork. And we drove on to New York City where we spent our first year.

The depression did not set in immediately after marriage; but the loss of all my old underpinnings of family and friends and locale was very hard to deal with in the sudden transposition of my life to New York. Morgan had a one-year assignment as educational secretary of a co-operative, and was gone all day. We had a makeshift home in part of an unrented apartment on the lower west side, furnished with the barest essentials. I assumed that I would not work! — a carryover from my mother's lifestyle which I had rebelled against but now re-enacted. So I spent a lot of time exploring the city, going to the World's Fair, and weeping with loneliness. After a few months I decided to do some volunteer work at a Neighborhood House; and then, after deciding to move to California, which was Morgan's home state, we packed everything in crates for shipping by sea, and rented a furnished one-room flat. That was a wonderful experience of freedom from possessions and housekeeping which I wish sometimes I could replicate.

I had also learned that it was essential for me to work. So I applied for a position as Student YWCA Secretary at San Jose State College, and Morgan volunteered to work in developing a co-operative store and gas station in San Jose, hopeful that in a year he would create a position for himself as director.

It was a creative year for me, working with Dr. Bertha Shedd Mason (who later became a Jungian analyst) as chair of the Board. But it was a stormy one for Morgan, who tangled with a left-wing faction on his own Board, and was not offered a position. Like so many wives over the years, I felt I had to break my contract with the YWCA in order to follow my husband to Los Angeles, his old home. It was an embarrassment. Not only did I have to leave my post prematurely, but I was ashamed that Morgan had failed to be accepted. I suspect that it marked the beginning of some disillusionment about the man on whom I had projected qualities that would ensure his ability to get along with all kinds of people: openness, a certain sweetness, willingness to risk, and a good mind.

The destiny that decreed our move to Los Angeles in 1940 opened many doors. Morgan's friends included four remarkable women who had been to Germany to study with Dr. Fritz Kunkel, and who were sponsoring him to come to Los Angeles as a refugee from Nazism. These were special people in my life who are known to many who may read this chronicle, so I would like to name them: Elizabeth Boyden Howes, Fay Allan (the Y.W.C.A. Secretary at U.C.L.A.), Lucille Nixon, and Frances Warnecke Horn. Dr. Kunkel would need a part-time secretary, and these friends arranged for me to have that job. They also had spent summers at Lake Minnesing in seminars on the Records of the Life of Jesus with Dr. Sharman. Morgan had been there too, portaging in by canoe for the six weeks of study, and he suggested that I go to a three-week version in the El Capitan mountains of New Mexico with Dr. Fred Howes as leader. This I did. And so it was that two paths opened for me that were to color the rest of my life: the study of Jesus, and then of Kunkel's work, leading to Jung. As I realize the momentous significance of that unchosen move from San Jose, I marvel at what Liz Greene described as the "something " which seems to know what an individual needs, or is going to need, for her unfolding.

Why follow these paths? Both areas of study helped me to find a religious and psychological "ground of being" from which to make choices, and I had not felt grounded. Dr. Elizabeth Boyden Howes, who has carried forward the study of The Records for more than fifty years, writes:

> The outcome of this search for one's own total value has been variously expressed through the ages in all cultures by religious men and women, by poets, by philosophers, and by scientists. They have used such expressions as finding and living through the "inner light", finding the "divine spark", the "Kingdom of God within", the "Self",

or such terms as self-actualization, wholeness, the integration of the personality, individuation. Jesus of Nazareth's consciousness about the incarnation process, coupled with his loyalty to the Jewish God of history, found expression 2000 years ago. It has been C.G.Jung in our time who has also confirmed the realization that as well as in the historical moment the highest value lies in the human psyche.[2]

And so it was that in the summer of 1941 I chose to travel to New Mexico for my first seminar on Jesus. The journey through New Mexico was my first experience of the American southwest, and as I relive it I feel the old excitement. I travelled across the desert to Albuquerque by bus, and then drove with the rural postman over a high plateau to the El Capitan mountains. I was his only passenger, and from time to time he stopped to take a shot at a jack rabbit. It felt a little like a western movie! After some hours I got off in a little town and was met by someone from the seminar to drive to a resort hidden away in a valley.

For three weeks we met daily, morning and afternoon, to examine the first three gospels to try to recover the authentic teachings and experience of the man Jesus. Again I quote Dr. Howes:

> The life and teachings of Jesus...offer a paradigm of a life fully and vitally lived in relation to a central value and an inexhaustible source for the clarification of choice-making. This approach is taken with the conviction that the life model and its source must be seen historically, i.e. as closely as possible to the way Jesus himself saw them, amplified by the findings of contemporary depth psychology, particularly that of C.G.Jung. The insights of the religious psychologist, Fritz Kunkel...are also included.[2a]

It was, and is, a rigorous study, demanding concentration and the letting go of old assumptions and stereotypes with which I had grown up. I was challenged and inspired. I felt as though for the first time I understood something of what Jesus meant by "the kingdom of God", and what was involved in making a commitment to "do the will of God". I felt that I made that commitment. To express

---

[2]Guild for Psychological Studies: *1993 Seminars*, Four Springs, California.
[2a]*Ibid.*

in words what that means is to oversimplify, but I will try. As I have experienced it over the years, it is to agree, in the presence of the One who cannot be named, always to choose mindfully, with as much consciousness as one can muster, to do what seems "right" for oneself and others and the planet. It is an *a priori* commitment, which is what makes the decision powerful and a numinous experience. The struggle is then to discern what feels "right" from this perspective; once seen, the choice has been made.

Fred Howes was familiar with the work of Fritz Kunkel, for whom I would be working in the fall, and that psychological approach illuminated the study of Jesus. Since Kunkel became such an important figure in my life, perhaps this is the moment to say something about this remarkable man. He was a medical doctor from Berlin, who after losing an arm in World War One, turned to psychiatry. In some 1936 lecture notes I find his remark that: "My psychological father is Alfred Adler...My grandfather, his father, is Freud." But Kunkel had rejected Freud's conception of mind as determined; and Adler's focus on individual conscious goals. Instead he moved toward Jung's recognition of the unconscious, of teleology (being drawn toward an infinite goal), and of the religious nature of the psyche. In a lecture series at the First Congregational Church in Los Angeles, (undated, but some time in the 1940s) he defines his work thus:

> My own endeavor has been to find the common denominator between Alfred Adler's "Individual Psychology" (which is not depth psychology) and the Jungian "Collective Unconscious". This common denominator I hope to have found in what I call the "We" experience. This experience, which we realize consciously, for instance, as love and sympathy, directs unconsciously the movements of groups and nations.

Unlike Jung, Dr. Kunkel's lectures and books focus on developmental issues in practical living, and on self-education with a view to living from the Center. By self-education, he meant "the powerful striving of a person to reach a higher degree of maturity...[which] means the integration of more and more unconscious functions and capacities into our individual consciousness."[3] One of his best-loved books is titled *In Search of Maturity*.

---

[3]Fritz Kunkel, *op.cit.* Most of Dr. Kunkel's books are now out of print. John Sanford, a Jungian analyst who studied with him, has published an anthology: *Fritz Kunkel: Selected Writings*. Paulist Press, 1984.

Over the last fifty years I have made the study of The Records three more times through the Guild for Psychological Studies at Four Springs in California, where the same material is examined in the light of Jungian psychology, and with greater understanding of the role of the unconscious in our spiritual life. The experience of Four Springs is the subject of a later chapter.

The trip back to Albuquerque began another lifelong friendship with Peggy Pond Church and her husband Fermor, who at that time lived in Taos, New Mexico, in a traditional house a hundred and fifty years old, with beaten earth floors. Peggy's father had founded the Los Alamos Ranch School, and Fermor taught science there until the property was commandeered by the United States government for the atomic research project that produced the bomb. Peggy was a published writer and poet, and later lived in Santa Fe until her death not long ago. I visited her there many times, for we shared both the Records study and a deep interest in Jung. Her legacy to me is rich indeed, not only in the many volumes of poetry, the book, *The House at Otowi Bridge* , and her letters, but her notes on the teaching of the Records seminars which she had led in New Mexico.

In September 1941 Morgan and I began a new life in Los Angeles, he on a teaching fellowship in economics at UCLA, and I as secretary to Dr. Kunkel. We had a combined income of $125 a month, rented a duplex bungalow for $30, and seemed to live well! Fritz Kunkel was the most far-reaching influence in those years because he introduced me to the work of Jung. In a recent issue of *Psychological Perspectives*[4] Gilda Frantz writes about those days in Los Angeles, and remarks that "Fritz was the kindest and gentlest person I had ever met." I concur. Fritz was now at work on a new book, *Creation Continues,* a psychological study of the gospel of Matthew. Since English was still difficult for him, part of my task was to assist in editing. He was evidently wanting to incorporate some of Jung's ideas in his writing, and I will never forget the day he handed me a large volume entitled *The Psychology of the Unconscious*, and asked me to "make a dictionary of the symbols". It was Jung's 1912 work, now published as volume 5 in the Collected Works and re-titled *Symbols of Transformation.* For someone unfamiliar with the realm of the unconscious, and for whom Jung was an unknown, this was an overwhelming challenge. How I managed to fulfill the assignment, I

---

[4] *Psychological Perspectives*, Issue 31, Spring/Summer 1995, p.15.

don't recall. But I was sufficiently inspired, and when life began to be stressful I turned to Hilde Kirsch, one of the Jungian analysts recently come to Los Angeles with whom Fritz himself was working.

In the two years that I worked for Fritz I met many interesting people, among them John Sanford, an analyst in San Diego who has recently published an anthology of Kunkel's writing. There were also evening gatherings in Dr. Kunkel's home, with guest speakers from many parts of the country. There I was introduced to the realm of psi and multi-dimensional reality. I met Agnes Sanford, a gifted spiritual healer; and Eileen Garrett, a well-known psychic. Later I came to know a Mrs. Barnes, whose trance sessions brought teachings from an unseen realm. I was also part of a small friendship group, one of whose members did automatic writing. We met once a month to listen to Marjorie Lang channelling "the WW's" whose words of wisdom were recorded. I only became sceptical when their comments seemed to echo a very right-wing point of view rather close to Marjorie's politics. But all this led to later reading, and still later to an interest in shamanism. What the physicist Fred Alan Wolf hypothesizes as a "parallel world"[5] has expanded my sense of the cosmos a hundred-fold over the years.

In the spring of 1942 my mother died. I flew home to Vancouver, my first plane ride, and joined in the plans for the funeral. When the undertaker wanted me to "view the body", I recoiled and refused; but later, at the cemetery, I finally broke down into uncontrollable weeping. That was the only mourning I did. I had written regularly and dutifully, long newsy letters to the woman who had been bed-ridden at home for a year and a half, slowly dying of the inoperable cancer. But the heart connection had been so damaged that I had no feeling of missing her in my life. It took long and painful analysis in my sixties to recover a sense of the real woman, my real mother, buried under the stereotype of an unhappy housewife, and to be thankful for her patient and generous love for me.

I am sad that she never lived to see her grandchildren. I had been pregnant when she died, but miscarried, and Reed was born over a year later.

I returned to my work with Fritz Kunkel for another year until my pregnancy with Reed was well advanced, and afterward we kept in

---

[5]Fred Alan Wolf: *The Eagle's Quest*. New York, Simon & Shuster, 1991; and *The Dreaming Universe*. New York, Simon & Shuster, 1994.

close touch. I am indebted to Dr. Kunkel for his friendly encouragement when I was having difficulty with breast-feeding. All I needed was someone to bolster my self-confidence as a mother.

Morgan's close friend, Fay Allan, lived in a magnificent old Spanish house with a Mrs. Ralph Smith, a woman whose generosity reached out to everyone, including this young Canadian wife, now a mother. Reed was born in 1943. I remember an art class in her home, where I created a clay figure of a woman with her breasts in the back, and burst into uncontrollable sobbing. Soon after that she offered me the gift of a paid consultation with Adelle Davis, the famous nutritionist. Later, when my second son, Frank, was a baby, I took him to Adelle Davis for advice about feeding, and she put him on her favorite formula of brewer's yeast and wheat germ. He did better on that than on the doctor's limited diet of milk and pablum.

Fay Allan's assistant was Lois Crozier, who lived only two blocks from our house, with her sister. She often came to dinner, and finally asked if she could be a "paying guest" because she hated to cook. That was fun for all three of us. Later, Lois married George Hogle, and worked in Jungian analysis with Frances Wickes in New York. Divorced, she now lives in a beautiful country home in Palo Alto where I have visited her. It is a friendship maintained over the years, even though we do not correspond, and when we met a few years ago at a seminar on shamanism in Colorado we had a delightful reunion.

Another new friend was Lore Zeller, who also lived close by. She and Max had come as sponsored refugees after Max was miraculously released from a concentration camp in Germany and fled with his young family to London. Max later became my analyst, but in those first years it was Lore who coached me in my new experience of motherhood, and together we walked our small charges in their buggies. Lore later managed the new bookstore at the Los Angeles Jung Institute, and is still (in 1995) in charge there.

All of these people became important in my life, enriching it with perspectives new and stimulating for a young woman from a conventional Canadian background.

A year later the depression began, gathering gloom as I became pregnant once more, and, as depressions can do, destroying all joy in doing anything. Once a person is stuck in that black hole, it seems as though nothing can help. It is one of the most difficult psychological problems to deal with, and the analytic work with Hilde Kirsch was not productive. Fifty years ago it would never have occurred to either of us to seek an anti-depressant to take the edge off the gloom so that psychotherapy could be useful. I went to her office dutifully every week until one day she "forgot" my appointment, and I never went back. In retrospect, I know that the early analysts who had worked with Jung had not had clinical training, or indeed any experience in working with troubled marriages. The approach was strictly with dreams, and I don't remember whether I was remembering my dreams. I was surely a difficult patient for someone just beginning a practice. Over the years Hilde Kirsch gained a reputation as a gifted analyst, and founded the children's clinic in Los Angeles.

After a few months, desperate, I began analytic work with Max Zeller, who also became famous in later years. We worked together for a long time, sometimes fruitfully, sometimes stalemated. He, too, was a "classical" analyst; and as the depression lifted somewhat I was able to profit from his deep understanding of the archetypal realm. But the marriage relationship continued to be unsatisfying. It is difficult, even now, to pinpoint the source of the distancing between Morgan and me. There were certainly many factors, one of which was that I was clearly unprepared for married life, and had no experience of children. I am sure that when I met Morgan all I really wanted was affection and companionship, but in the thirties people didn't just "live together". I had been groomed for professional life, bolstered by leadership experience, Mary Bollert's confidence in me, and my training to be a dean of women. That line of development had been cut off prematurely — but I had no real awareness of what was happening.

Part of the trouble was certainly our increasingly different focus in life — Morgan's preoccupation with social "causes" such as Henry George's taxation proposal, and the movement for World Federal Government (which I have since supported) and mine with depth psychology and religion. Until there was some healing within, it was impossible for me to contribute to the outer world. Morgan had had no further interest in the Quakers after we left Pendle Hill, and he was disdainful of Jungian analysis. Most of all, perhaps, was a blocking of feelings on both sides. There seemed to be no room for my own growing as a person. I needed to "come alive" and the relationship stifled that need.

Also, my inability to take pleasure in mothering was dismaying to me. The early struggles with my own mother, and the absence of expressiveness and play in that first family, left me without a model. Analysis seemed not to help very much in these two areas, but it did begin to give me a sense of my individual self, and it inoculated me, as it were, with a deep appreciation of Jung and the dream life. That never left me; and through the years, wherever there was space in my active life, I turned to Jungian literature for inspiration.

When the children were small, Morgan's mother, Elfrida Greenfield Harris, was a great support. She loved me, and did her best to relieve the strains in the household. For periods of time she lived with us, at one point having her own apartment contained within a duplex that we had remodelled into a single family home. She had a sense of play, and knew how to spend time with the children in ways unknown to me. I remember that she believed in fairies. My last image of her, many years later when I went back to Los Angeles to study, was a serene, white-haired little woman in a nursing home, completely happy that she had such delightful journeys in astral travel.

When the boys were old enough to be in a wonderful preschool called Child House, I searched for a part-time job. I was qualified to be a YWCA secretary, but felt I couldn't handle that kind of responsibility. So I drew on my early skills in sewing and brashly applied for a position as seamstress in the Lanz workroom where they created custom-made clothes of an Austrian peasant style. The woman who interviewed me was Hedy Holt, who later told me that she hired me because she liked me! — not because she felt I had enough experience. Lanz was a small store with the kind of family atmosphere where people celebrated birthdays by bringing a cake to share with the entire shop. And in the workroom we had some wonderful discussions. There were five of us, coming from Austria, Germany, Japan, Canada and the American deep south. Sometimes the discussions grew so heated that we would all have stopped sewing, and then Hedy would clap her hands, and say, "OK, back to work!"

Most importantly, Hedy and I began a lifelong friendship — one that Morgan did not share. Hedy had grown up in Austria in a large musical family, and as a young woman had taken a course in dress design and pattern-making. When the Nazis invaded Austria her family had had to flee, but not before most of her brothers had been detained for periods of time, one of them in Dachau. She and her husband, Fred, managed to get to New York with only ten dollars in pocket, and Hedy found a job as a lace-maker. Eventually they came to Santa Monica, and when I knew them they were living as an extended family in a huge old Spanish house in the canyon. They had brought her parents from Austria, and the youngest brother, Walter. Another brother, Herbert, who had been conductor of a symphony in the Philippines until politics drove him from there also, now lived nearby with his wife, a dancer. I loved to be among them, and was often invited to Sunday tea where Hedy served Viennese pastries she had made from ground nuts, butter, eggs, chocolate — no flour! Utterly delicious! There were also wonderful evenings of chamber music. Their son, Henry, grew up to be conductor of the Opera in Seattle, and their daughter, Lucy, to be a professor of mathematics at Tufts University. Such a family was a totally new experience for someone who was an only child on both sides of her own family.

Still another enriching friendship was with Eleanor McClurkin, who became the sister I never had, someone with whom to relax and share intimacies when tensions piled up. She was extraordinarily intuitive, almost a shaman, and through her I met Dr. Charles Vouga, a Swiss psychologist who had come to California to do research on psychological and spiritual aspects of astrology. When Eleanor met him she began dreaming of the mathematics of astrology — something she knew nothing about — and she and Charles began a collaboration which continued after he returned to Paris, until his death. For me, astrology proved to provide clues to my inner and outer struggles to be my own person, and Eleanor, as long as she lived, used to comment on my current chart reading on almost every birthday. Frank, my son, learned astrology from Eleanor, and also discussed my chart with me — a process which brought us closer together as adults.

The time frame of all these friendships was the 1940s, the period of World War Two. There were other friendships, these with men, which became intimate with Morgan's encouragement. He felt that my conventional upbringing was part of our problem, as indeed it was; and that sexual freedom might lessen the repression and help the depression to lift. It is hard to evaluate his attitude, unusual as it was and is. For me, it felt like an endearing kind of non-possessiveness which I respected. When I later became engaged to Fred Buckland, I was able to extend a similar generosity toward Fred, who had a very dear older woman friend whom he didn't want suddenly to abandon, and whom I was able to accept. With Morgan, the experiences lessened the tension and provided a kind of learning whose timing was misplaced: they would have been more appropriate *before* I plunged so hastily into marriage. They had the effect, I think, of merely postponing an inevitable separation.

Indeed, the skirmishes within the marriage were increasingly alienating. Our paths began to diverge when the children were preschoolers, and we separated from time to time when I couldn't stand the tension. One summer I took the small boys to my father's ranch and stayed until it was clear that my depression was too much for my step-mother. In Vancouver I was reunited with old friends, and when the time came to return to California, I didn't want to go. But I

Langdon Frank Harris & Morgan Reed Harris, c.1947

wasn't ready to be on my own with two children to support. That took a long, long time — eighteen years in that marriage. At one point we asked a counselor who had spent some weeks in our home, to listen to each of us, singly and together, and give us her opinion. Finally she said to me: "Clare, do you love Morgan enough to compromise your desire for your own life in order to stay married?" And I had to answer, "No". But I still was unable to leave.

During this period there were also financial ups and downs. Morgan had been teaching economics at a small college, but grew restless in the conservative Christian environment and left to work with a powerful politically conservative man, Frank Burke, at his radio station. Morgan's right-wing sympathies surfaced at this time and I was uncomfortable with the extreme anti-communism. This was not the man I thought I had married. The radio work came to an end, and with it our income. So I found a Christmas season job clerking at I. Magnin's on Wilshire Boulevard. *That* was an experience! During a sale I was sent upstairs to ladies' fashions, and inadvertently waited on someone else's customer. For that sin I received a dressing-down from the regular saleslady, including criticism of my dress and my unshaven legs. I was humiliated. The manager of the gift department where I usually worked was a Canadian, and had taken a liking to me, and when the season ended he offered me a position in the personnel department. I was flattered, but not interested.

The United States was now at war, and in the summer of 1942 the Japanese were being evacuated from the coast. I had a two-month assignment from the American Friends Service Committee to interview students for relocation in eastern colleges. I felt their distress and the injustice of the situation deeply. I will never forget asking the Dean of a university faculty for a transcript for one student, and being told abruptly that he would never assist one of "those damn Japanese". When it came time to make my report to the A.F.S.C. committee sponsoring the service, I met Helen Satay [I'm not sure of her present surname] but she is an unforgettable figure. Helen became interested in me, and later, in 1954, when I decided I *had* to have some time alone away from the family, she found a job for me as executive secretary to a young contemporary architect, William Beckett, whose office design had won an award. The salary was $300 a month — more than we had ever had! And I discovered the world of contemporary design, feasting on the international architectural journals that changed my taste in furnishings forever.

Searching my files recently, I came across a letter from a mid-life counselor, Paul Povlsen, whom I had consulted when applying for this job. Having been out of public life for so long, I was anything but confident that I could manage work in the world. I remember that Dr. Povlsen had me write small essays about my life, which he would then critique for signs of low self-worth, of which there were many. He must have helped me with my letter of application, which is also in my file, for it sounds totally confident! His letter, dated

December 5, 1953, written after I had been accepted as William Beckett's assistant, is gently encouraging:

> Please remember from this experience that if you truly know your objective and go after it intelligently nothing can stand in the way of achieving it. Nobody is trying to keep you from it and forget outer appearances or how impossible it may seem of arriving there.

We arranged a temporary separation in December 1953 and I moved out of our home and celebrated my fortieth birthday, feeling that indeed, "life begins at forty". We arranged for Reed to live temporarily with a family in the country where he had spent two summers at camp, and we placed Frank in a boarding school. When that proved an unhappy place for him, he lived for a brief time with Morgan until I had had some respite from the tension. Except for moments when life opened up for me, it was a lonely and miserable time for everyone in the family.

That was when Morgan and I both began bioenergetic therapy with Dr. Curcuruto, and for the first time in my life I began to experience feelings that were genuinely my own, rather than trying to feel what I as a "good girl" *should* feel. The process was slow and painful, but absolutely crucial. When I later became a therapist myself, I appreciated that in cases of repressed spontaneity body therapy is a necessary accompaniment of insight therapy. *Both* are necessary. Still later, when I studied communication as part of my doctoral dissertation on family educational programs, I realized that in addition to feeling one's own feelings, it is important to be able to express them. Keeping them to oneself maintains repression and stalemates relationships. Carl Rogers' development of "active listening" and Tom Gordon's work on "I" messages are both creative additions to psychotherapy.

Both analysis and body therapy helped me to know myself better, but I still did not feel free to leave the marriage. Fate — in the sense that Liz Greene describes it as the "something" that knows what is necessary for our growth — did not let me off the "hook" that bound me to Morgan. What I had to learn was that compassion can be a trap for me...not compassion in the deep Buddhist sense, but sacrificing oneself in order to be helpful to a person seen as "needy", without recognizing one's own neediness. Knowing myself better was not enough; I had to come to the place of loving myself. And more. The releasing factor came unexpectedly one day on the telephone. My friend Eleanor had called me at work to share the pain of her own marriage, and I heard myself quote Fritz Kunkel: "If the universe is a unity, then what is good for one person must be good for the other; and what is bad for one person is bad also for the other." I had heard that about fifteen years previously, but was not ready to understand it in relation to my own marriage.

I went home that afternoon, knowing that my decision was made, and that I had to communicate it to Morgan. It seemed simple: neither of us was happy, we were both compromising our own growth in order to stay together. It wasn't working. It wasn't good for either of us. While it was clear to *me*, and I had a job and enough confidence to feel I could support the two boys, it was not that easy for Morgan. He had never let go of his wish to have me in his life, and after a period of separation, and in one last try at "making the marriage work", he had moved into the house I had been able to buy. But he had no secure income; he had many interests that occupied him, but no sense of vocation. Both of us were still working with Dr. Curcuruto, individually, and I remember vividly the session in which I clarified my sense of what made the marriage untenable. I said to Dr. Curcuruto by way of summary: "I love Life, and Morgan doesn't".

As I write that statement, I realize that it sounds like a harsh oversimplification. What lies behind it, I think, is the spiritual trust in Life's processes, the acceptance of Erik Erikson's concept of Integrity vs. Despair. In "Identity and the Life Cycle" he wrote:

> It is the acceptance of one's own and only life cycle and of the people who have become significant to it as something that had to be and that, by necessity, permitted of no substitutions...and an acceptance of the fact that one's life is one's own responsibility.[6]

I had not read Erikson at the time, nor could I have verbalized my simple affirmation as clearly. What was at stake for me was what I had told Louise Bray in that counseling session seven years before: I cannot compromise myself in order to stay married. I now had to break the Gordian knot of false compassion. Morgan and I had at one

---

[6]Erik H. Erikson: "Identity and the Life Cycle". *Psychological Issues,* Vol.1, No.1, 1959. International Universities Press, Inc., New York.

point in the separation agreed on divorce, and what remained was to finalize the interim decree. This we did in the spring of 1958.

By that time I was working for the Santa Monica Community Chest as Assistant to the Director, and beginning to know that my vocation did not lie in that kind of work, although the director had indicated she wanted to retire, and asked if I would like her job. It is significant that Fate brought a new opportunity as soon as I had freed myself to move on. A letter came from Janet Mitchell, one of my teachers at St. Clare School and now one of the seven Founders of York House School, asking if I would be interested in returning to Vancouver to be headmistress? Mrs. Clarke was retiring and they were seeking a replacement. I was surprised, and flattered. How did they ever think of seeking me out? Would I fly up for an interview? Yes, I would, and I did.

The image of that glorious April spring in Vancouver is still vivid: the rock gardens and flowering trees, and the soft rain. I had lived in California for eighteen years, and not quite realized how I missed the gardens, the sea, and the mountains. Even the rain! It was coming home. I accepted, and became the second headmistress — except that I preferred the title, Principal. I then had to return to California to wind up my life there.

Thus began a new era. Not without strain for my sons, who were twelve and fourteen, and having to move far away from their father. It was particularly difficult for Reed, who was just finishing junior high school and wanted to move forward with his buddies.

For the boys as well as for their parents, Fate had decreed stormy weather in their early years. I can't imagine anything more forlorn for tiny children than to have a mother so depressed she can't express caring. That is my greatest sadness. And they must have felt abandoned in the short period when I left to have time alone. Frank was in an art class at that time, and over and over drew detailed pen and ink sketches of a man about to walk off a cliff. Perhaps Morgan, with whom he was living, was suicidal; but the eight-year-old must have internalized his father's despair in addition to his own suffering.

As soon as I had found an apartment with a bedroom he and Reed spent weekends with me. For a while we joined a club for field trips camping and bird-watching, and the boys enjoyed the family groups. All through their elementary school years the period *after* school was the worst for all of us. There was no child care at school, and the small boys were on their own. Every single working mother knows the anxiety this produces. We managed to finance bioenergetic therapy for them, and I remember their therapist saying to them, when we were moving to Vancouver, "Your mother is the only one in a position to take care of you". They had no choice.

I *wanted* to "take care of them". They were a gift to me out of that marriage, and I loved them, even if inadequately. As I became happier and as they grew up, we could share more of our feelings. But they were understandably angry that I worked so hard, and had so little time to be with them, especially in their high school years while York House demanded so much of its Principal.

And so we sold the house on Lindenwood Lane and travelled to Vancouver in July 1958, caravaning with a friend and his children. By an irony of fate we were spared the destruction of that lovely house in a fire that swept up the canyon a year later, wiping out six of the seven houses on the cul-de-sac. The money from the sale was to finance our home in Vancouver.

The Clare who journeyed north that April was a very different person from the depressed woman of five years before. I had learned to take initiative in the world, experiencing a new kind of masculine energy. And the feminine had blossomed through many creative friendships and the love of an old college friend, now widowed. That relationship was not to evolve into marriage because he needed a homemaker for his children and I needed to grow through a professional life. But my feeling side had come to life.

The story of the York House years is a tale unto itself.

"Three Generations", Morgan, Reed and Michael

69

YORK HOUSE

Our arrival in Vancouver on that summer day in July ushered in a whoie new era for each of us. For me, the six years at York House School for Girls were some of the happiest in my life, even though they ended in exhaustion. They also included my marriage with Fred Buckland, whose love evoked my feminine self as never before. And I think my father was happy that in some fashion I had returned to his world of values. He never understood my ideas about education, but he was proud of the achievements that brought recognition. I felt I had managed, for once, to please him.

For me it was coming home. For Reed and Frank, thrown into a whole new environment, it was more difficult. Of the two, Reed perhaps suffered most. To enter high school as a stranger to country, city and neighborhood is an enormous challenge, and Reed rebelled. By the end of the first year he had become depressed and developed diabetes. The psychological component manifested in dramatic fashion. When we went back to Los Angeles for our July vacation, Reed worked with our old homeopathic chiropractor with the result that at the end of four weeks his intake of insulin was reduced from sixty to five units. And within two weeks of returning to Vancouver, it shot up again to sixty. At school the rebellion took another form: he hated Canadian social studies and failed it twice, quite deliberately. I think the happiest time was in his final year when he switched high schools and became involved with a group learning to waltz in a very professional manner. Much later, this same interest led him to enjoy a more interpretive type of "Contact" dancing in pairs.

Frank, who had not been as happy at junior high school as Reed, seemed to find the change a somewhat welcome challenge. But he was bored with high school and decided to gain advanced standing so that he could graduate in three years instead of four. The final push was a course at summer school, and he achieved his goal. I think this approach to a difficult situation is typical of Frank, and has manifested itself most remarkably in his parenting. Not having had a happy childhood, he told me he was determined that his own children would not suffer as he had. Even though his first marriage ended unhappily, he has given devoted attention to all his children, and enjoyed them.

Reed, by contrast, has found fathering as difficult as I found mothering. And typically, the diabetes has involved bouts of depression. As with me, his sense of vocation is coming late in his life, and perhaps he, too, will have more to share with his children as they grow older.

We were welcomed to Vancouver by Janet and Howard Mitchell, who opened their home to us until we would find one of our own. Janet, as I said, was the one who wrote inviting me to apply for the position of Principal. She had been one of my especially loved teachers in high school and we had become friends. She contacted a real estate agent, and we looked at house after house on the west side, not happy with any of them. Finally, I said, "You know, I think the trouble is that we are used to a California style house, and that is what we really want." "Well", the agent responded, "there has been just such a house on the market for six months, and the owners withdrew it because nobody liked it!" By that afternoon she had gained permission to see this unacceptable house, and I fell in love with it immediately. The boys were not so sure at first; they liked one with a basement room that would have been their very own space. But they finally agreed, and we bought it, with the help of a loan from Auntie Grace for the second mortgage. Typical of her generous self, she later cancelled the loan note, converting it to a gift. The house was on the corner of 28th Avenue and Camosun Street, facing St. George's School for Boys, with a lovely fenced garden. That made it possible to have Frank's little dog, Scamp, shipped up to join the family.

The Camosun house was home for all of us until Scamp was critically injured and both boys had finished university. When I left for graduate study at UCLA in 1968 I rented it, and then when I returned to California for a post-doctoral year I sold it, thinking I might never be back. Typically, I made the decision unilaterally, not even discussing it with my sons, who were then in their twenties. It was a decision I later regretted, for I did come back, realizing that Vancouver was "home", and for all three of us there was then no ground to share. Apartments never felt the same.

In mid-August I began my duties at York House. There were some formalities to learn — like wearing a hat! I had to buy one for the reception at the Grauer home on The Crescent given as a farewell for Mrs. Clarke and a welcome for me. In the picture I look very strange. All the years in California were hatless; and now Mrs. Clarke admonished me that it was mandatory to wear one in public. I remember that I usually left it on the back seat of the car, in case of need.

The car! That is a story too. In Los Angeles I had bought a 1946 Ford convertible, used, as my very first "own" car, for the grand sum of $150. It was pale blue, with dark red leather-like upholstery, and when we decided to move north, I had it painted slate gray. It looked like new, and was valued at $550 by the Canadian customs. It still had California plates, and attracted the attention of traffic officers because I was used to driving much faster than Vancouver allowed. It also attracted the attention of young boys, who would accost me when stopped at a corner, and shout, "Wanna sell it, lady?" A convertible has always spelled pleasure and freedom for me, and I still own one — the third generation.

I think the girls at York House also saw it as a symbol of their young and "different" Principal! Looking through my file of clippings from that first year, I came upon a newspaper interview which reads:

> At first, one concludes that Mrs. Harris is an improbable principal for a girls' school — that is, if one is old-fashioned enough to regard private schools of this type merely as seminaries for the appropriate upbringing of young ladies.
>
> As a matter of fact, I made the initial mistake of referring to her as a headmistress. This, she gently pointed out to me, she is not. She is the administrative head of the school...
>
> Mrs. Harris is no school marm. She is slightly above medium height, a pleasant, soignee, highly articulate woman

with lively blue eyes, an urbane manner, and an extremely business-like approach to the problems confronting her.[1]

The "problems" were for the most part challenges to do things totally unfamiliar to me. The first was a staff meeting. I had never taught school, although I had taken an observation course in Education and a seminar on "The Foundations of Education" at Teachers' College, Columbia. Now, I had to present myself as someone able to organize and give leadership to an entire school, kindergarten to Grade 12. Intuitively, I ended the session by saying: "I will need your help", and apparently that was the right note to strike. The teachers were experienced, and in a transitional period they were glad to feel that their own ideas would be valuable. The school had been founded in 1932 in the depths of the depression by a group of seven women with a vision for a truly Canadian girls' school. As long as Mrs. Clarke was Headmistress she had been the Authority, and had governed with assurance and wisdom. Now, clearly, something new was to be born as the parents took over ownership and governance.

I inherited a proud tradition, and was succeeding a Headmistress and staff who had followed a vision of a school created "Not For Ourselves Alone", which is the motto of York House. The newspaper clipping (undated) quotes Mrs. Clarke as saying that all schools that strive for wholesome living and education will continue "as long as we do not lose our idealism." "She believes", says the interview, that "private schools are able to exert a quiet control not possible in our public schools...Her students are trained for a useful life." The headline reads: "Respect and Affection Her 'Farewell Gifts'".

I suspect that by temperament and life experience, and as a woman of the next generation, I brought to my position a different viewpoint about authority. I had rebelled against my father's dictum of "absolute, unquestioning obedience"; and I had lived in California for eighteen years. A philosophy that had never been articulated slowly took shape.

The first evidence was my approach to morning prayers, held as an assembly for students and staff. I inherited from Mrs. Clarke two small books of prayers, one of them Anglican, plus the tradition of reading from the little red volumes of Psalms and New Testament

---

[1] *The Province*, Saturday, March 21, 1959.

Clare Harris, Principal of York House School, c.1959

provided by the Gideons for each girl in the school. The written prayers didn't feel comfortable for me, who had grown up in the United Church and later joined the Society of Friends, the Quakers. Also, I was very aware that York House was not officially a "Christian" school, and that many students were Jewish. I wanted a more universal approach — and where to find resources? One day, driving on Tenth Avenue, I spotted the Wayside Pulpit of the Unitarian Church, and on it a quotation from Emerson. Aha! I immediately made an appointment with Dr. Phillip Hewett, the minister, and borrowed some of their Sunday School materials. What a rich discovery! I began attending the church, and soon joined, beginning what has been a marvellous experience for me to this day.

From then on, I collected beautiful bits of poetry, philosophy, science, sacred writings from all parts of the world, and began writing my own prayers. Soon, I decided to have separate assemblies for the Primary, Junior and Senior schools, since each age group would respond to different expressions of the religious impulse. And I tried to coordinate the prayer with the hymn and the reading, to carry through a theme. This became for me one of the most rewarding aspects of my contact with the students, and many alumnae and staff have mentioned their appreciation of those morning prayers. When I left the school I had two volumes of collected writings which I lent to one of my successors, but morning assemblies no longer include this aspect. I remember that during my tenure there was a Royal Commission on religion in the schools, and I attended one of the hearings and urged that there be some inclusion in the curriculum of universally inspiring poetry and philosophy, without ever being sectarian. We are more and more one world, and the approach to the spiritual dimension in every religion needs to be part of our education.

In this same domain, the Christmas carol service was always one of the highlights of the first semester. Marie Gerhardt-Olly, who was one of the Founders and the Vice-Principal, directed the overall presentation so that it would have dignity and that the girls would do the readings beautifully. And the girls sang like angels! These services were held in St. John's Shaughnessy Anglican Church, and parents and grandparents packed the hall to capacity... On the morning that school closed for the Christmas holidays we also had a special candlelight service in our own gym. That, too, became one of my favorite events. The girls brought items for infants in far-off lands to put under the Christmas tree, and we lit candles in my large candelabra one by one, with a special reading for each. As we closed with Silent Night, the lights were gradually dimmed until only candlelight lit the hall — a truly beautiful moment.

That first Christmas, at the close of the service, the girls brought me a gift — a large square box wrapped in white tissue. When I opened it, out leaped a tiny grey kitten, terrified by the shout of joy from two hundred girls! The old and loved custodian, Ludi, who had been at York House for nineteen years, came up to me and offered a name: the Duchess of York. When the kitten proved to be male, he became the Duke of York, or Yorkie, a treasured addition to our family. The next Christmas, I thought to take him back to show the girls how beautiful he had grown...which he did not appreciate. After the service, he disappeared, and I went up and down the block and the lane, calling, with no avail. When I returned, discouraged, to the office, we found him up on the highest shelf in that dark, safe spot.

The sequel to that story is that when I was finally able to get another cat, after many moves, I found a beautiful long-haired gray cat, a stray, and he is Yorkie the Second. As an indoor cat he is more sedate and less venturesome. The first Yorkie used to follow my husband, Fred, and me on evening walks, even in the snow.

As the first term progressed and I found myself in many situations requiring some articulation of a philosophy of education, I turned to a little booklet by Rudolf Dreikurs, published in 1952: *Character Education and Spiritual Values in an Anxious Age*.[2] There I found my own concerns echoed — concerns that I expressed in monthly Newsletters to the parents, and which were certainly controversial. I was trying to move toward a wider distribution of responsibility for behavior so that the girls would internalize the values which the school upheld, rather than being bound by rules. Dreikurs writes:

> The democratic atmosphere requires social and personal values different from those found in an autocratic society...Proper stimulation must replace pressure...(citing Kurt Lewin). [First], under autocratic leadership children behave well, but display great hostility to each other when out of reach of the controlling leader. In contrast, the children in a democratic group operate with each other as well within the supervised group activity as outside it. Second, while it was not difficult to change a democratic atmosphere into an autocratic one, bedlam broke loose when the autocratic group atmosphere was changed to a democratic, *until the youngsters learned to take on responsibility for their group activities* (emphasis added).

---

[2]Rudolf Dreikurs: "Character Education and Spiritual Values in an Anxious Age", Boston, Beacon Press, 1952.

Looking back, I think the word authoritarian would be more appropriate than autocratic. What struck me was the emphasis on rules. I recall an incident one morning that first September as Mrs. Clarke and I walked past a classroom and a Grade 9 girl asked me if they could have permission to hold a rummage sale. I turned to Mrs. Clarke to ask what was usual in this respect, and she simply said "Certainly not" and walked on. I felt uncomfortable; my style would have been either to discuss it, or to say, "Let's talk about it later. I don't have time right now."

But the transition from one style to another was difficult for everyone. The school grew fairly rapidly, especially at the high school entrance level, and the new students coming from public high schools had no experience of York House traditions of behavior. That put increased onus on the prefects, who had major responsibility for enforcing things like dress code, and on staff for being "firm" as well as friendly. Kurt Lewin's observation was accurate, even though the shift in attitude was gradual. When I look back on the rigidity of the dress code, it seems clear that we should have relaxed it, instead of trying to uphold a style of uniform that has since gone the way of "bloomers" and berets and white gloves. I hate to think of the energy invested in concerns about items already being abandoned by most women except on formal occasions.

In the spring of my first year the decision was made to accept boarders. So the Board of Governors suggested that I should make a tour of cities in the interior of British Columbia, and in Alberta. And I had my picture taken for the press — a picture that is still my favorite because I look so supremely happy. I was enjoying my work, and feeling loved and appreciated.

Pressures increased with the arrival of boarders. Some of us had had experience of being a boarder, but no one had foreseen the extreme difficulties of hiring residence staff to look after twenty-two junior and senior girls away from home, some of them very unwillingly. They came from as far away as Hong Kong and Pennsylvania, and although we had two excellently qualified women in charge, there were many problems.

Dr. Peter Spohn, a member of the Board of Governors, was a great help not only in cases of illness, but in being available for counsel. When he died, tragically, it was a great loss. And when Margot, one of his daughters in grade 10 at the school, died in a skiing accident, we mourned doubly. I don't recall much of what happened otherwise

77

in the residence, but the venture was not deemed a success, and we abandoned it after one year, to my great relief.

There were other new programs much more rewarding. In fact, the freedom to initiate new projects was one of the great rewards of being Principal. Moreover, the parents were enthusiastic and supportive. One of their contributions, in collaboration with the alumnae, was the formation of the Women's Auxiliary, which over the years has sponsored fund-raising through the annual Yorkshire Market. The Newsletter in March 1964 reported that over five years they had raised $13,200 which had provided teaching aids, furniture, books and scientific equipment. They had also organized a uniform exchange.

Nineteen sixty-four was a banner year. We opened a new senior school building, the first to be designed specifically as a school. Until that time, with the exception of the gym, we were housed in beautiful old homes along a full block on King Edward Avenue. We rejoiced particularly in properly equipped science labs, a large art room, and an assembly area which we named Founders' Hall.

That Hall holds some vivid memories for me. One is of Morning Prayers when the Senior School assembled and two hundred voices rang out in the great hymn set to Blake's poem "New Jerusalem", with a thundering piano accompaniment which only Hilda Langridge (who taught piano) could have managed... Another is the afternoon of John F. Kennedy's assassination. It is hard to realize now, with our historical déjà vu, the hero worship accorded John and Jackie Kennedy in the 1960s. The noon radio accouncement caused near hysteria among some of the girls, and the staff urged me to call an Assembly at 1:30 to dismiss school. Later, in that same Hall, we gathered to watch the funeral cortege on television, sharing in the mourning.

Another project was the introduction of a French bilingual program with the aid of funds from the Vancouver Koerner Foundation for two successive years. In my May 1964 Newsletter I commented:

> Since their funds are limited, and in great demand, and they rarely give a grant a second year, we may feel highly complimented by their interest and faith in our project.

The money was used to bring a teacher from Paris, Mme. Irene Roland, who taught regular curriculum in arithmetic and geography from Grade One to Six, plus sessions with kindergarten. The idea had been sparked by a brain-storming session with a few Board members, wrestling with the need for students to begin French early, and to speak it well. The problem had always been lack of time in the daily schedule. It suddenly occurred to me that if some of the regular curriculum could be taught in French, this might solve that problem. The idea is standard procedure now in French immersion classes, but in 1962 it seemed to us revolutionary.

The project received considerable public atention. The Grade Two children who were doing arithmetic using Cuisinaire rods (another innovation), were invited to demonstrate at UBC Open House. Clearly, they were thinking through their operations in French, not translating, and it was impressive to watch. The Vancouver Sun gave it a quarter-page picture with a long write-up.[3] The article reads, in part:

> The real purpose of the program is to have children learn elements of the actual curriculum in French, so that they can talk about real things, not merely storybook characters.
>
> We hope to build on each group's experience with French from year to year so that by the time they enter high school they will be ready for fluent reading and discussion of French literature and culture.

In 1962 I was President of the B.C. Association of Independent Schools, and I had long wanted to host a new kind of meeting. My first one, back in 1958, had been strange, indeed. We were only a handful of "Heads", but we sat in straight chairs, arranged in rows, and there was virtually no discussion. Nor had there ever been a gathering of staff from all the schools. Few of the teachers at that time were members of the B.C. Teachers' Federation, and there was no program of staff development. Since this was a time of ferment and new ideas in education, I invited resource professors from the UBC Faculty of Education to come and lecture or demonstrate to all staff members. One hundred and fifty teachers came from all over the province. The response was tremendous, and the feeling tone enthusiastic. We were able to meet in the new Founders' Hall, and to have people tour our new building as well as the Junior and Primary

---

[3]*The Sun*, Thursday, May 14, 1964, p.45.

classrooms which were still housed in two of the homes on the property. It was a celebration.

That same year the Board gave me a grant of $500 to attend the Canadian Conference on Education in Montreal, and then tour some of the fine independent schools in Montreal and the eastern United States. It's hard to imagine that sum of money financing such a trip, but it did. The clipping from The Province, March 2, 1962, states that

> Mrs. Harris would be looking for more flexible approaches to individual learning. "Any type of organization or method which allows the student to proceed on her own ability." Measurement by test rather than creativity is something she deplores and she is a great believer in the no-ranking report card. Mrs. Harris sums up her educational creed thusly: The measure of greatness of any institution is found in the effectiveness with which it discovers and fills human needs. She firmly believes even the privileged must toe this line.[4]

I wish I had some journal notes of that trip east. The visits to schools were an inspiration and encouragement to me, even though for the most part they evoked dreams far beyond the reach of York House. One of the visits was to a high school on Staten Island, New York, where a college friend, Kay Would Amaro, was a specialist in reading. She gave me many ideas for a remedial reading program that we were able to adopt in part. It was the vision of democratic styles of governance in the Quaker schools in Philadelphia and New England that reinforced the philosophy that was part of my own innate style.

There were other ventures too. I wanted the girls in Grades Seven and Eight to have some information about sexuality, and Dr. Lydia Tyhurst, one of our parents, agreed to give instruction, with parental consent. The Family Service Agency made possible the further development of a demonstration project in sex education by contributing the time of one of their staff, Jean Assimakos.

Also, I wanted the Grade Twelve girls to have some experience of volunteer work in the community, in order to be better informed about social problems. Again, the Family Services Association pro-

---

[4]The Province, Friday, March 2, 1962, p. 21.

vided a grant to allow Mary Rupp to meet with the Community Service Club, and to lead students on field trips.

Each class in the senior school had had one period a week of "Religious Knowledge" instruction, and I wanted to broaden the study beyond traditional Bible study. The most valuable change was at the Grade Twelve level, where Mrs. Gerhardt-Olly began to teach comparative religion.

This is the moment, I think, to comment on the role of this remarkable woman whom the Grade Twelve girls revered, girls from every class back through all the years. She had various titles: academic head, head of the senior school, vice-principal, Mrs. G-O. But it was her wisdom, humor, and breadth of knowledge and vision that captured all our hearts. She had been my teacher in high school, later and always my friend, and a very significant mentor. From my tribute to Mrs. Gerhardt-Olly on her retirement, here is an excerpt:

> Who else could mean so many things to so many people? Approachable by the tiniest child in nursery school, infinitely understanding when one has a problem, wise, with a breadth of knowledge seldom found in an age of specialization, lightening the tense moment with a twinkle and a story, blessed with the patience of Job to encompass the follies of us all...who else but Mrs. G-O can be firm and loving at the same time?...Mrs. Gerhardt-Olly knew so well that to teach is to open doors, to probe and encourage her students, to demand excellence, to cajole, to share.[5]

Over the years our friendship deepened, and as I move into my eighties Marie is one of my inspirations. As she grew older she lost her beloved husband, Gerry, and gradually became blind. This meant moving out of her home into a care-giving residence. And health problems became acute, first with a pacemaker for her heart, and then with kidney dialysis. Yet throughout this period of increasing limitation she never complained, listened to talking books and to media discussions of world affairs, and was always eager to discuss ideas with those who visited. She is indeed my mentor for creative aging. Her death brought great sorrow; I still miss her.

---

[5]The York Rose, 1994, p.29.

With so many new developments my own excitement ran away with me. More and more new ideas whirled in my head, and I didn't realize that I was pushing staff too hard. One day Marie said to me, quietly but with exasperation: "Clare, slow down. It's too much." Because I loved her and respected her wisdom, I was able to hear that warning. Perhaps I would not have heeded anyone else. I'm not sure what year this was, but already there were signs that "the quiet control" which Mrs. Clarke had spoken of was breaking down. Not all senior students were capable of taking, or willing to take, the responsibility for their behavior which a democratic structure requires. Conservative parents criticized the relaxed rules. The Board of Governors didn't want staff or student representation at their meetings, as I had suggested, and there were few women on the Board to balance the viewpoint of many of the corporate executives. I met one of these women the other day at the market, and she said: "You know, I often think of those days with sadness. You were a philosopher, and the parents wanted a disciplinarian." And the Board didn't want so many changes.

I recall, for example, one of the men going over the budget of staff salaries with me and suggesting that teachers should be paid by the hours they actually teach! He objected to my re-structuring responsibility by appointing a senior teacher in each division to be "head" of that school unit — a plan that greatly enhanced the smooth running in each building.

By that time I had met and married Fred Buckland, who when he saw the list of Board members, exclaimed: "No wonder you are having problems!" Some of the problem was of course my own. In my last year someone loaned me Virginia Satir's book, *Conjoint Family Therapy*,[6] and I realized that I had neither skills nor experience in sitting down with everyone involved in a conflict, to negotiate a solution. Often I had found that a student, her teacher, her mother, and her father, each had a different perspective and contributed new information. But it had never occurred to me to gather them all together to discuss the issue. Nor did I have at that time Carl Rogers' listening skills; and I'm sure that I projected onto some of the men on the Board my experiences with my father, who belonged to their world. Later, when I returned to graduate school, I did some work

---

[6]Virginia Satir: *Conjoint Family Therapy*. 3rd Ed., Palo Alto, Calif., Science & Behavior Books, 1983.

with Virginia Satir and much work on communication. It was not until I began analytic training that I worked in depth on the relationship with my father. Reading David Whyte's wonderful book, *The Heart Aroused*,[7] I am struck by his phrase, "future possibilities already mortgaged to past limitations". Yes, indeed.

So the last year at the school, 1964, was a difficult one. I grew more and more exhausted, suffering what today we would call "burn-out". In January I had to take a brief leave in order to rest, and my February newsletter carries the comment:

> It was very gratifying to know that the overall organization at York House, with its decentralized plan of three departments under three Directors, was so sound and in such good hands that everything ran smoothly in my absence. Those who share in the leadership of the school — Mr. Carley as Vice-Principal, Mrs. Gerhardt-Olly, Mrs. Norminton, and Miss Hodgson as Directors — are all doing outstanding jobs. And I think one could not ask for a staff more genuinely interested in the progress of individual children than is ours.

The saddest incident of that final year occurred after Easter. Two Grade Twelve students brought liquor to the school in their lunch thermos, and drank enough to be slightly drunk. I sent them home and said I would consult about their punishment. There was an absolute rule against alcohol on the school grounds, and the penalty was expulsion. I felt strongly that that would be unfair, considering their long years at the school and imminent graduation, but I had to have staff support. Summoned to a special meeting in the staff room, they unanimously agreed that the rule must stand. Even Mrs. Gerhardt-Olly felt it was a matter of principle not to give way. Dismayed, I went to talk with their class, asking if they would help me devise an appropriate penalty. Again, I could find not a single vote for lenience. Back in my office, I broke into tears. This did not feel right. I knew the Board would not support an exception; indeed, they refused to discuss the matter. To this day I ponder how I could have acted differently. Perhaps in 1964 there was no other way. Today community service can sometimes be an alternative to punishment.

---

[7]David Whyte: *The Heart Aroused: Poetry and the Preservation of the Soul in Corporate America*. New York, Doubleday, 1994.

There was one terrible meeting with the Board when the Chairman cut me off as I tried to present my report. I stifled tears, and got up to prepare tea. My resignation followed. With a heavy heart and stoic control I presided over the graduation ceremonies in the gym, unable even to respond to Mrs. Clarke when she took my hand and led me down from the podium to say her own appreciative and tearful farewell. I had turned to stone to defend against sorrow. It was all I could do to sing the final "God Save the Queen". All the next year, I grieved. So much idealism, so much creativity, had gone into my work as Principal that it took a long time to "let go and let it be".

In my files I found the text of my farewell address to the graduates, and I include it here because it sums up poignantly all the idealism wrapped up in those years at York House.

> You who graduate this year will leave, as others before you, with memories too varied to express, with the sense of an era closing behind you and a new, uncharted road ahead.
>
> Always we who have taught you wonder what you have really learned from York House. What does our School stand for? What is inherent in its spirit which gives it life, and breadth, and depth?
>
> Perhaps our Christmas Closing Prayers put some of these values into words. You will remember that we light candles celebrating our unity as a school, our love for the Light which dwells in the hearts of men...candles representing Truth, Love, Thanksgiving, Understanding, and Faith. On your behalf your Head Girl lights a candle honoring the Laws which govern our school community, reminding us that from the two great commandments to love God and to love our neighbor stem all the imperatives of justice, of orderliness, of cooperation with others in the interests of the whole. NOT FOR OURSELVES ALONE do we seek to be law-abiding, but that we may learn to become citizens of the world, committed to the love of God and the establishment of one great family of man, at peace with one another. The candle which it has been my honor to light for York House for five successive Christmases, I have lit with the deepest affection, with pride, and with humility. We need to remind ourselves constantly of the

vision of our Founders as they established York House thirty-five years ago. They wrought steadily to establish ideals of integrity, of initiative, of individuality, of responsibility. They hoped to arouse intellectual curiosity, and the willingness to tackle difficulties with disciplined minds, the ability to love and to be loved.

If we cherish these ideals, if we seek constantly to express them in our individual lives, if they govern our decisions and guide us in the solution of our problems, then York House can continue to evolve into the great school we envision. The dream itself may be purified in the endeavor; the outward form may change; those invested with leadership may come and go; but the dedication must remain. The identity of York House is a precious thing, commanding our loyalty through stress and triumph alike.

To our graduates, to the staff and students who carry on these traditions, and to our parents, I point again to this imperative which must compel us all: to strive always for a clearer perception of Truth, and a more active love of Good. The quality of our success and of our happiness will be a by-product of such devotion. As I, too, leave this cherished place, the same challenge impels me forward. I need to learn, and I wish to serve. May God bless all our endeavors.

6

FRED

The great gift at this time was Fred, who had come into my life in December of 1961. Doris and Frank Applebe introduced him, and in the Christmas vacation some of us, with our teen-age children, went skiing to Penticton, a town in the interior of British Columbia. Fred had a summer home on Lake Skaha, and I remember sitting with him on the beach by the lake, building a small bonfire, and talking. He was a tall man who walked with a sure step, enjoying life. He had a shock of white hair, and blue eyes that looked at me with a straight gaze. His hands were huge, and carried the marks of the woodsman he was.

Some of our first encounters were jarring, but Fred persisted and his genuineness won out. A year or two before, he had fled one night from one of the endless tirades in his marriage, and never returned, so we had to deal with "unfinished business" and negotiations for a divorce. It was a bitter struggle, and some of our conversations turned on the lines from Edwin Markham's little poem that ends with: "Love and I had the wit to win; we drew a circle that took [her] in." He was hurting from the letters from his younger son who had been co-opted into the attack, and there had to be time for healing. His own native gentleness helped.

The snapshots taken at Christmas a year later reveal my joy in this relationship. When Frank saw one recently, he remarked: "You look so happy there!" Fred's love, like Mary Bollert's, was unconditional, and my feminine side blossomed in a way utterly new for me. We moved slowly toward any sexual expression, not just because of my public role but through a sense of timing on Fred's part, as if wanting to savor each step. And that felt right for me, too. This was not a "love affair" but a growing partnership.

There was a delightful "engagement" dinner in Seattle with some of the women leaders from Four Springs who were there to give a seminar. They bought us a giant margarita at Trader Vic's which we shared with two straws, happy pair that we were.

We married over a year later, at Easter. I finished writing report cards on the Friday when school holidays began, and almost knocked Fred down in my joyous rush to hug him as he arrived back from work at a forest reserve. "I'm finished!" The wedding was in the Unitarian Church, with Beethoven's *Ode to Joy* sung as a hymn instead of the usual wedding march. My old friend, Eleanor McClurkin, who was by now my assistant at York House, was Matron of Honor. The angels sang with us.

Fred was a forester, with a natural woodsman's love of the trees, and renowned skills in hands-on work in the forest. He held an honored position in his company, but did not want to move into a city administrative position, feeling that he belonged in the woods where he found his inspiration. I have recently re-read the sermon he gave at the Unitarian Church on "Our Forest Heritage". It is a beautiful piece of writing, full of his delight in that world. I want to share some paragraphs.

> This is a creation that has been since the world began, a continual renewal of life, a cycle of growth and decay. Life is dependent on death, and death with decay leads back to life and growth. The process is continuous, with beautiful results, and all of it in harmony. It is this harmony, I think, that is the most impressive to the mind of man. The order and the change without confusion. The myriad variety of living and moving things. The co-relation of the plants, the insects, the birds and the animals.
>
> A shaft of sunlight comes down through the tall trees, illuminating a white mushroom pushing up through the dark forest soil. A spider's web is stretched, high in tree branches and miraculously constructed in two planes, flat, in a world of three dimensions among the intricacies of branches. A fern frond is slowly opening, a beautiful

light green contrasted with all the other darker green shades. Over near a wind-fall log is a packed run made by forest mice. It is barely discernible, but you can see where fir cones have been stripped, much as we strip an artichoke, and the seeds eaten.

Suddenly there is a brilliant flash and a whirring sound, and a humming bird appears, investigating a honeysuckle flower coming from a branch entwining a jack pine. Everything you see is a different color, and there are many scents and sounds. These myriad forms of life are all fulfilling a different function, many complementing each other. This living forest, changing but everlasting, is to me one of the proofs of order in our universe. I see in the forest not logical and relentless evolution, but the hand of a Creator working forward to a design that is at once pleasing, beautiful, and excitingly stimulating. The hummingbird epitomized my thoughts in this regard. It is so frail, so beautiful, so amazing in its actions, so surprising when seen in its forest habitat. To me, it is not logical that this creation has merely evolved. Evolution is obviously part of the process; but I suggest there is also the work of a Power with a beautiful imagination.

It is the peace and serenity of the forest that I find most helpful. As you learn to enjoy the forest, you become aware of the forest. It somehow complements your subconscious thinking so that you become aware and relaxed, rather than alert and tense. You become a part of something that is harmonious and meaningful, and through this process your mind can become more receptive so that our peculiar process of thinking has a chance to be creative.

This was the man I knew and loved. The dilemna for us was that Fred didn't want to be working out of town all week and home only on weekends; he wanted to be with me. Just at that time, the B.C. Institute of Technology was opening, and they invited him to join the faculty. This he did. Unfortunately, neither of us realized that his was not the kind of organized, strategic mind that would find classroom teaching and library research compatible. He was much more the poet. Indeed, some of his co-workers remember his reciting po-

Alfred Channing Buckland, c.1960

etry when out in the woods. At B.C.I.T. he almost immediately felt like an alien and began to lose confidence. The administration offered to shift his assignment from classroom to field work, which seemed to make sense. But it wasn't a solution, and depression set in. At Christmas he resigned.

Almost immediately he was offered other jobs, both on the mainland and in Victoria. It was too late; the loss of confidence destroyed the wonderful natural assuredness he had had as a man totally competent in his field. I watched, and supported, and we had one wonderful vacation on the Olympic Peninsula, chasing and playing games on the sandy beach. I suggested therapy, sure that this one failure could be overcome. We tried many approaches, including hypnotherapy in Seattle, but nothing helped. The psychiatrist later told me that Fred seemed not to have the ability to utilize psychotherapy. Finally, the doctor advised shock therapy, and alas! Fred did undergo that treatment. He became subdued, without his usual vitality; and when he took an assignment in the woods, found that he had even lost his intuitive orientation to moving around in forested areas. It was devastating.

After another brief time as an in-patient he seemed somewhat better, and we tried to resume some semblance of a normal life. We even went to a U.B.C. Alumni dance, Fred looking handsome as always in his tuxedo and red cummerbund. Although not his exuberant self, he seemed to enjoy the dancing. That was a Saturday night in November, 1965. We had been married two and a half years.

On Monday evening I went over to the church to lead a group on The Records of the Life of Jesus, leaving Fred sitting at the little desk in the den. In the midst of our study group, all the lights went out. And when I got home, Fred was missing. Frank reported that he had taken the little VW bug and gone out — he didn't know where. At midnight he had not returned, and I called the police. They found him the next morning, parked in the nearby cutoff through the woods. He had died from asphyxiation.

He had written a note, telling of his despair of recovery, his knowledge that he would end up in a mental institution. He didn't want that for himself, or for me, whom he loved. He had drawn a spiral winding down to a point, and then opening wide again in an upward movement. That was how we both understood death.

That morning, unable to stand the tension of uncertainty, I went over to the church where I was working as Phillip Hewett's assistant. Frank was at home studying, so it was he on whom the burden fell of receiving the news, and phoning me. Fortunately, Phillip was in his office, and I took the news to him. After talking with me for awhile, he asked if there was a friend I would like to be with, and I said, "Marie". So he drove me to her home, and it was into Marie's arms that I collapsed, weeping. She and Gerry comforted me most of the day, and then phoned Eleanor to come and drive me back to get my car, and follow me home.

Friends moved quickly to give support, as friends do, and people at the church were also wonderful. Two friends who were members went into the woods and brought back a moss-covered log and greens to decorate the church for the memorial service. Eleanor gave the eulogy. My father came from Victoria, and I was deeply touched that my stoic father broke down and cried. He had grown to respect and love Fred, and had been so glad for my happiness. I broke down too as we sang the last lines of the hymn which had been Fred's favorite.[1]

> Then break the silence with a voice of praise
> Before we fall asleep, before we die;
> Press mind and body hard against this world;
> Open the door that opens toward the sky.

The wonderful woman who had been my secretary at York House, Isabel Swainson, came to the house and took care of a host of details, including the multitude of notes of sympathy. I was numb.

And not only numb. In the shock and grief I "lost myself" for a long time, unconscious of what I was doing to avoid the pain. The first unreal move was to flee from the grief and do what seemed my responsibility: to go to a meeting in the United States of Family Service agencies, in my capacity as the newly elected chair of the Board. Later, I resigned, and paid back the money given for my expenses, for of course I was useless as a delegate.

The more serious act was to avoid grieving — not knowing then how essential it is for us to give ourselves a long, long time to mourn a loss. Since I was Assistant to the Minister at the Unitarian Church, I moved into what felt like a genuine stance of "overcoming", turning to philosophy and religion for faith and strength to believe with Camus: "In the midst of winter, I finally discovered that there was in me an invincible summer."

On February 17, 1966 — three months after Fred's death — I actually conducted the service at the church and entitled it: "The

---

[1] "Now Give Heart's Onward Habit Brave Intent". Words by John Holmes, in *Hymns for the Celebration of Life*, Unitarian Universalist Association, Boston, Beacon Press, 1964.

Shaking of Personal Foundations". I talked about building one's house upon a rock, and said:

> If there has been a prior commitment to this way of life, before the shock of whatever tragedy has befallen us, this commitment can have tremendous holding power. Out of sheer self-respect one feels a necessity of honoring one's own voluntary agreement to live in accord with an ongoing evolutionary principle, wherever it may lead us. The unbearable experience *is* unbearable in the moment but something deep within us knows that we have the power to work towards acceptance and growth. There is also the need not to let others down. Our close friends can endure our despair but they need to know that we are fighting to move to a more affirming level. The lifelines we extend to each other need to be grasped and used.

I don't remember any feedback from this sermon. My feeling today is that I was not being helpful to anyone, let alone myself. It would simply make it harder for others to honor their grieving in appropriate ways. And the sequel for me was a blind descent into darkness masked as a new beginning. I was not to recover from this madness for a long time. That story belongs in another chapter.

As time went by and I tried to understand the whole story, there were many facets I needed to recognize. The first was my own naive idealism. I genuinely believed that nothing was impossible with love and motivation and intelligence. I didn't acknkowledge limitations, the natural boundaries of the givens of personality. This was 1965. My brief training in counselling was three decades in the past; Jungian analytic study more than a decade in the future. I still had much to learn about the opposites potentially present in what is seen as positive. This tragedy was one of the impelling factors in my search for alternative tools for healing.

Secondly, I had to recognize that although Fred sacrificed his position as a forester in order to be with me, his traditional way of working was already being overtaken by technology, and his firm's presumed willingness to make a place for him in the city, at Head Office, would not have been congenial to Fred, either. The challenges of change were just around the corner, not yet encountered. Fred was a man caught in the dilemmas not only of love, but of modern work life.

Life at home was not always peaceful either when Fred first joined the two boys and me. As every "blended" family knows, the system is shaken. Reed and Frank were in university, and loved to discuss and argue over dinner. Fred was temperamentally no match for them at this purely intellectual, rational level, and I often shared his discomfort. The scene reminded me of my own altercations with my father when I so certainly "knew" what was so. But I think Reed, in particular, suffered from Fred's death, for he had spent time in the forest with him and had found in Fred a father figure whom he genuinely loved. His own Dad was still somewhat distant, physically and emotionally. It would be some time yet before both young men would reach out to know and love Morgan.

* * * * *

It is now thirty years since Fred died. The joy and the pain have become an enduring part of me, an experience of profound love, and tragic loss. I remember an Easter Sunday, driving to church and recalling our Easter marriage...tears of overwhelming gratitude for the gift of that love trickling down my face. I think he must have been hovering nearby. Unconditional love creates a dimension of inner confidence and grace that never die.

7

LOSING AND FINDING

If you bring forth what is within you
What you bring forth will save you.
If you do not bring forth what is within you
What you do not bring forth will destroy you.

Jesus
The Gospel of Thomas
Gnostic Gospels

I was fifty years old when I left York House in 1964. Midlife. David Whyte writes of midlife as a time when "the whole weight of our existence shifts on its axis...For every man and woman, midlife is a pivotal time of internal rebirth."[1]

Before there can be rebirth, there must be a death — the death of the old ego and a new connection with the Self. This chapter is about that dark passage, the time Dante describes as "a dark wood where the true way was wholly lost."

September of that year had marked the beginning of a year of rest and exploration, and time to be with Fred in a more relaxed way. I was granted permission to audit some classes at U.B.C. and particularly enjoyed anthropology with Michael Ames, now the Director of the Museum of Anthropology. Later that fall the shadow of Fred's depression fell across our lives and I had less heart for studies. But I felt the need to be occupied with something creative, and Phillip Hewett and I worked out a plan for part-time work as his assistant at

---

[1]David Whyte: *The Heart Aroused: Poetry and the Preservation of the Soul in Corporate America*. New York, Doubleday, 1994, pp. 181, 208.

the Unitarian Church, at a nominal salary, beginning in the fall of 1965.

The church had become a place of inspiration for both Fred and me, and I was drawn to learn from Phillip's breadth of mind and knowledge. He is a tall, slender Englishman, very much an intellectual, a gifted writer and preacher who reads poetry magnificently. When I first knew Phillip he was very shy about expressing feelings — something I understood very well! — but, like me, he participated in encounter groups and became more relaxed with people. I remember that I once had a dream of him entering my home as a shaman, with antlers on his head. He was my mentor in the area of spirituality. What I wanted to bring to him, and to the church, was my experience with Jungian writing and with the study of The Records of the Life of Jesus.

Fred seemed well enough that summer that I could leave for two weeks to attend another seminar with the Guild for Psychological Studies, refreshing my memory of The Records in order to lead a study group. Eleanor McClurkin, who was close to Fred, kept in touch with him, and he was also working in the woods from time to time. At Four Springs, in the art periods, I sculpted two pieces that spoke of Fred. One, done mostly with eyes closed, became a kneeling androgynous figure that carried the symbolism of both the inner marriage of feminine and masculine, and of my union with Fred. This I have kept all these years. The other was a portent of danger: the figure of a woman with a storm raging at her feet, as if the water might engulf her.

Three months later Fred had died. The stormy waters of the unconscious did indeed damage for a time the ability of the conscious ego to discriminate. Our unconscious side contains both positive and negative potentials, and if our conscious life is lop-sided toward the ideal, as mine was, there is danger that the negative will overwhelm us. Warnings come in nightmares, or in spontaneous art work such as the raging storm. Those menacing waters were a symbol of that aspect of my own unconscious. When the ego does not pay attention, we fall into unconsciousness, as I said in the Preface. We lose our awareness or intuition of what is required of us on the Journey toward wholeness.

What happened in the following spring of 1966 was the work of the Something that knows what is necessary for our growth, as Liz Greene wrote. It was a descent, falsely seen as a brave new beginning.

My work at the church involved counselling and conducting church services when Phillip had to be away. It was also an opportunity to create new structures in response to need, as I had so enjoyed doing at York House. One of the new ventures was a lunch-time program for seniors, The Daytimers. They still meet twice a month, with some younger members arranging for speakers and helping with serving tea to accompany the box lunches. I spoke to the group occasionally, and attended their discussions — lively discussions, I might say! Unitarian elders are known for their continuing interest in the issues of the day and for many individual talents.

One day a message came that there was a man outside wanting to speak to me. He didn't want to come in, but wanted to set up an appointment to talk to me in my office. It was Alex Earle, a short, well-dressed Englishman who seemed to have fallen on hard times. We did talk on a number of occasions, and we became friends. I tried to involve him in some of the activities of the church, and since he had a good speaking voice I invited him to share in the reading at the dedication of the tapestries which a group had been weaving for our new sanctuary.

He also took part in one of the workshops I had organized for the three leaders from The Guild for Psychological Studies who came from San Francisco to introduce The Records to three small groups. Two of them, Dr. Elizabeth Howes and Dr. Sheila Moon, also gave sermons at the two services on Sunday morning. Alex was in the group with the third leader, Luella Sibbald, but not very interested; and he was possessive of me in the lunch hour which I found annoying. We had become more and more involved, but there were bothersome moments that I tried to overlook. At lunch with Elizabeth Howes I spoke of this friendship, and Elizabeth cautioned me to be wary. She felt he was superficial, and that it was too soon after Fred's death for me to risk a relationship. How right she was. But I couldn't hear. My despair at the thought of being alone forever drove me into a belief that it was courageous to risk loving again.

Blinded by this stance, I loaned Alex $1500, and helped him furnish a bachelor flat where we spent time together, secretly. I talked about him to no one except Isabel and Barney Swainson, who responded to his charm and humor. At least some part of me felt this quick new relationship was "wrong". Nevertheless, I plunged on. We decided to take a long trip and I told Phillip that I could not renew my contract, that I needed to get away. Once that was decided, I took

Alex over to meet my father and stepmother in Victoria — at which point Alex complained of eye irritation and began to wear dark glasses.

When we discovered that the ship to Japan required a marriage license in order for two people to share a cabin, we married secretly in Bellingham in May, 1966. Isabel Swainson was our witness.

I conducted the church service on the following Sunday morning; and at two o'clock we left by bus for San Francisco to sail to Japan. I had paid for the tickets. Eleanor was to rent my house for an indefinite period. The ship was wonderful, one of the President line, and we met a young Japanese woman, Yuko Naito, a survivor of Hiroshima, with whom we became friends. She invited us to meet her later in Hiroshima, which we did. We also had an introduction to the elderly Japanese minister who had founded a Unitarian fellowship in Tokyo; and an invitation to visit a Unitarian minister in one of the northern villages where he had started a day-care center. The trip held lots of promise.

We arrived in Yokohama on a hot, humid day in July and took three taxis and two inter-urban trains to Tokyo. I have a vivid memory of wearing a pink linen suit, much too warm, of my ankles being swollen, and of struggling with our huge suitcases up and down endless flights of stairs. Once there, the ryokan —the traditional Japanese inn — was a delightful experience, especially the hot deep bath, with a little wooden bucket for splashing water that drained away on the sloping floor. Japanese breakfast with raw egg, miso and vinaigrette salad was another matter; we decided henceforth to walk over to the Imperial Hotel for an English breakfast.

I thought I had lost the newsletter about our Japanese experience, but to my great delight it turned up in a folder in my file, marked To Keep! The tone is one of delight in people and places, a sense of happiness that had since faded because of the miserable ending of the Alex story. How easy it is to color our experience either black or white. In our two weeks, the journal reads,

> We travelled to many out-of-the-way places where people obviously saw few foreigners and spoke little English. But we came to feel completely at ease because everyone was so friendly and helpful, quick to smile and bow or to offer a seat on a crowded commuter train.
>
> One of the happiest evenings was a return to the Tivoli — a little pub — where Alex played the piano, cheered on

by the young audience who kept asking for Dixieland jazz. A young man sat near the piano with us, kimono-clad, and sang in French, imitating Louis Armstrong!

Dr. Shinijiro Imaoka, a member of the International Association of Religious Freedom and President of the Japan Free Religious Association, invited us to go to the Sunday service of the Tokyo Unitarian church, even though it would be in Japanese. Dinner with Dr. Imaoka was a charming and memorable event. He took us to a tiny restaurant, unmarked, off a side street, where in a private room we sat on cushions on the floor, and were served by two young girls who obviously loved and respected Imaoka-sen-sei, the venerable scholar of eighty-six so young in spirit. The cook faced us, preparing tempura until we could eat no more. I had a terrible time trying to sit comfortably, squirming endlessly as we ate and talked. Our host spoke quietly of his concern for true freedom in religion, and told us about Rissho Kosei-kai. Later he escorted us there and introduced us to Dr. Negu who gave us two beautiful volumes (in English) describing the temple and its many services.[2]

This is a most impressive liberal Buddhist movement, founded in 1938, and now housed in an enormous temple complex. The walls of vermilion jasper in the Great Sacred Hall were dominated by a golden statue of the Buddha. We were told that the Society served two and a half million families from birth to death in their various facilities, including schools, a hospital, an old people's home, and a training center for leadership. They are *laymen* who have accomplished this, based on a very simple, basic Buddhist teaching aimed at perfecting character: "by improving in knowledge and practice of the faith, by personal discipline and by leading others, we will endeavor to realize a state of peace for the family, the community, the country, and the world."(p.110)

I was impressed by the fact that they offer group counselling on a daily basis, and that they are a "movement away from exclusionism toward mutual respect and cooperation." (p.110) Their founder and president, Nikkyo Niwano, was invited as a special guest to the Second Vatican Council in 1965 and they are part of the Religious League of Japan which includes all the religions in Japan. I suspect

---

[2]*Rissho Kosei-kai*, Kosei Publishing Co., Tokyo, 1966.

that was why our Unitarian host wanted us to know about Rissho Kosei-Kai.

What I remember most about the trip to the northern town of Komagane in the Japanese Alps, is the train ride. It was summer, and Japanese families were in a vacation mood. They shared their fruit with us, and I watched young fathers playing with their small children. This was a new perception of Japanese men, who in my Vancouver experience were rarely expressive. The other intriguing fact was the food offered through open windows each time we stopped at a village station. I longed for a bowl of noodle soup, but didn't manage to negotiate it quickly enough. We also had to watch for our station, not recognizing the names in Japanese script. In fact, we did get off too soon, and spent the night happily in a ryokan beside an ancient temple garden.

The next morning we went on to Komagane, to visit the Shidara family. The Rev. John Shidara is the only Universalist minister in all of Japan, and their family story is one of tremendous courage and dedication. They fled from Tokyo three days before the final bombing in 1945, settled in Komagane as refugees, and in twenty years have developed a true community service center: church, meeting hall, day nursery for eighty children of working parents, adult education classes, and a clinic. When we arrived we asked in the little corner store for a taxi, mentioning Mr. Shidara. The taxi-driver already knew: any Westerner who comes to that village is looking for this beloved man.

The day care was a simple structure, colorful and well equipped, and the children were delightful. Alex, who could play almost anything on the piano by ear, sat down and played nursery rhymes, much to their delight.

After leaving Tokyo, we journeyed to Kyoto on the famous express train, watching for Mount Fuji, which hid in the clouds, and enjoying the efficient food service. Two images from Kyoto: The first, we sat on the tatami matting in a huge temple while three little girls tried to teach us some Japanese relative to their butterfly cage and net — after which we all ended up eating ice cream! The second, a young Japanese student wanting to practise English with us, led us through the gardens to his nearby home on a stream. Seated on the deck in the sunshine, he clapped his hands to call the carp, who came quickly. His mother bowed and smiled.

On the ferry across the Inland Sea to Hiroshima I finally managed to buy a bowl of noodles in miso, and was sitting struggling to negotiate the slippery noodles into my mouth when I looked up. There was Alex, with five young men, laughing at my predicament and all set to take my picture. I wish I had it! In Hiroshima we met Yuko and together we explored the Peace Museum, deeply moved. That night she wanted to share our room with us, and I'm ashamed to say that we didn't agree to this, not being at ease with that kind of intimacy. I feel the awkwardness of that moment, as I write. It would have been a friendly act, especially as she was inviting us to go with her the next day to visit a country spa way up a valley from Fukuyama, owned by relatives. We were the first Canadian visitors.

There we had a traditional Japanese meal with the family amid much laughter and translating of jokes. We met Yuko's mother, who spoke no English, but dressed in full kimono and obi performed a portion of the formal tea ceremony. And then a wonderful thing happened. We were invited to experience the communal baths — a series of three, with gradually warmer water. Alex declined, but I gladly donned the offered kimono and followed Yuko's mother to the pools. Laying aside our kimonos, she and I sat at the edge of the pool and began to soap ourselves. Everyone was naked, men and women together, but there was a sense of privacy. Suddenly the mother was soaping my back, and rubbing it gently, then splashing water over me from the little tub. I reciprocated — and felt a wonderful sense of communion with this diminutive elderly woman.

Back in Tokyo, I bought a beautiful gift for Yuko, and mailed it. But I never heard from her again. I'm not sure whether I violated some protocol around gift-giving, or whether she was somehow embarrassed by the gift. I felt sad for the lost connection. Her story was typical of the survivors of the bombing, and of the patriarchy. Her parents had been killed, and her adoptive father had refused to allow her to marry the man she loved, also a survivor. She was trying to support herself until she would be free to defy his control. That this could happen to a modern young woman with an M.A. in English from an American university puzzled me at the time, but is more understandable now. I find myself remembering Elizabeth Barrett Browning and *her* father's possessiveness that was clearly sexual in nature. Perhaps, additionally, Yuko was indebted to her father for her education.

So much for the Japanese experience, which was by far the most fascinating for me. We travelled from Yokohama to Sydney, first on a small ship stopping in at Okinawa and Hongkong where we stayed for a week. That, of course, was the place to buy silk and pearls and wonderful sweaters, and I had a marvellous time shopping. The strongest impression, though, was the poverty on the little side streets leading up the mountain, and the reaction of the woman who ferried us to the floating restaurant in Aberdeen. Clearly, she hated relatively wealthy tourists. And on shore some boys threw rocks at us. We were told of many reasons why the Chinese in Hongkong were resentful and unsmiling. For instance, so my newsletter reports:

> In mainland China rickshaws propelled by humans have been banned as degrading, but in Hongkong the Westerner expects to be transported thus. [I wonder if it is still so in 1995.] There were times when I felt embarrassed to be white-skinned, feeling the just resentment of the hard-laboring Asian for my affluence. This was especially marked in Aberdeen. Sleeping babies were everywhere strapped to the bent back of the boat ferrier, and young girls and boys openly begged for coins from the tourists on the plush launches of the guided tours. We always avoided tours and wandered among the crowds, but I wouldn't have dared to do so without Alex — the faces were too grim and tense, as if they thought we were idly curious, intruding on their poverty.

From Hongkong we took a British freighter with a Chinese crew, which made one stop at Brisbane. There, we only had time to take a bus to the park where we could see koala bears. My boys had had a koala as a loved cuddly creature, and I wanted to see them alive! What amazed me about Sydney was the devotion to sports: stores closed at noon on Saturday so that everyone could enjoy their favorite game, and every restaurant seemed to have a TV screen blaring the current soccer match. The now-famous opera house was not yet finished. The beaches were reminiscent of Long Beach on Vancouver Island, stretching for miles. Otherwise, I was not impressed, and felt alien to the spirit of the place. I think I was getting a little homesick, and wanting to head back via Europe, so we missed going to New Zealand, a foolish omission when we were that close.

In late August an Italian luxury liner was sailing from Sydney to Naples, and we booked passage. Three long weeks on the sea, at times turbulent in spite of stabilizers on this huge ship. I was sea-sick, like most of the passengers. And when feeling well dined alto-gether too richly so that most of my clothes became too tight. Also, I grew bored, and never wanted to see another ship. We couldn't land in Bombay because of a strike, and I was thankful to get off while the ship navigated the Suez Canal, take a bus into Cairo and spend a full day there. Alex stayed on board. In that brief time I managed to see some of the treasures in the museum, to drive out to the nearest pyramid, and shop. In the streets I marvelled at the tall, slender men strolling in their long caftans made of pale blue Arrow shirting, the folds swaying gently as they walked. I determined to make one for myself some day — and did. In one of the jewelry shops the owner bargained insistently for the I.Magnin wool sweater I was wearing, and I finally succumbed to a trade for a gold bracelet. By the time we got to Italy the weather was chilly, and I regretted the bargain.

Memories of our few days in Rome and Florence are of ancient beauty, treasure piled upon treasure, with few specific images to share. We went on by train and ferry to London, where I grew in-creasingly cold and weary and longed for home. Finally I decided to fly by myself, since Alex was afraid of planes, and he followed later by ship. Back in Vancouver I realized how much tension had been building, and to greet friends again was pure joy. I rented an apart-ment on Beach Avenue with a wonderful view of English Bay, and furnished it very simply with a few things from my house, still rented to Eleanor, and a few purchases. Alex arrived, and we de-cided to try to create a Coffee House modelled on some we had en-joyed in our travels. The first experiment was on Saturday evenings at the Unitarian Church, and it was a great success. Alex played the piano, people sang and read poetry, and we served various coffees and pastries. Hard work, but fun.

So we began to look for a suitable place to rent for a public ven-ture. Finally we found a store front with the right atmosphere in West Vancouver, and approached the owners for a lease. Alex didn't come to that meeting; I went with the real estate agent, and pre-sented our plan. The lawyer was stony-faced. I can still see his ex-pression as he looked me straight in the eye and said, "Mrs. Earle, we will never give Alex Earle a lease." I pressed him, even protesting that "I'm no fool!" "I know you're not, but we won't give Alex Earle a lease." He offered no explanation. The agent was silent as we drove back. When I told Alex, he simply said, "I suppose it has something to do with my credit rating, which may not be very good."

One other incident belongs in this picture. In the fall I had invited Eleanor McClurkin and Bill Willmott to come to dinner. Shortly before their arrival, Alex went out for a walk — and didn't show up for dinner. Around midnight a friend phoned from the Vancouver Hotel to say that Alex was there...and he arrived home about two in the morning. My anxiety was so high that I had asked Frank to come and stay the night with me, and Alex was annoyed to find him there.

I demanded an explanation, which he refused. Later, Eleanor told me that she was sure he was afraid of her strong intuitive sense, which led her to distrust him.

Frank remembers that around that time I "made quite a speech" about being too old to change my life! I had given up on dreams and settled for an ordinary life. Something in me had died along with Fred, and I was living an un-alive existence. I had killed feeling, and my whole personality must have had a numb quality. But I was not yet conscious of that. Frank was understandably concerned about me as he left to return to his teaching job in Mexico. I had not shared much with either son. Reed was living on his own, and our paths seldom crossed. He remembers little of Alex, except that he did not particularly like him. Like me, he had no experience with deceit and did not question Alex' lifestyle. The fact that I talked so little about what was happening seems to reflect some sense of embarrassment about this sudden marriage and flight into travel.

On the weekend following the real estate debacle Alex announced that he was going to drive up to Kelowna to discuss an insurance deal. He had not been working all this time, and now he needed to pursue his old business. I went to U.B.C. on Monday as usual, for I now had a position as administrative assistant to President McDonald. Days passed, and Alex did not return. I grew more and more puzzled. Finally, a friend of his whom I had entertained at dinner, phoned me. He had run into Alex at the bank on Monday, and Alex had told him he was sailing for Japan that afternoon. I was dumbstruck, still clueless. When I went to the bank I found that he had closed out the joint account which had been set up to invest in the coffee house. His safety deposit box contained the name of his former wife, and a birth certificate with a different name.

Shattered, I spent the evening with Isabel and Barney Swainson, who were enraged. A few days later, at midnight, the phone rang. An operator asked: "Will you accept a collect call from Alex Earle in Tokyo?" "No, I will not", said I flatly. "Are you Mrs. Earle?" a puzzled voice asked. "I am. But I will not accept a collect call." Alex then came on the line, contrite, wanting my forgiveness. Did I still love him? "Alex, I can't love a man I can't trust." That at least was clear to me. At work, I struggled to concentrate, trying to put all the puzzle pieces together. There were a lot of them that fit the picture of a "con man", had I had the eyes to see and ears to hear.

The friend who had informed me called again, to say that he was going east and would try to get in touch with Alex's wife. He felt sure that she had always refused to give him a divorce — which explained Alex's wish to be married in Bellingham. This the friend was able to do, and brought back her telephone number. My lawyer managed to reach her and hold her on the phone long enough to vent her rage and exclaim: "I will never give that son of a bitch a divorce!" He then prepared a document stating that my marriage was disqualified — and I was free to return to the name Buckland, which I loved and felt I had dishonored.

The woman who had declared defensively "I'm no fool!" had indeed been a fool. My father wrote flatly, that I *was* a fool; I had poor judgment. This letter was in response to a tearful, embarrassed one from me, and I was hurt that he had to rub it in, and told him so. Even my stepmother admonished him for being so hard on me. But the rage and the shame were acute, and I had to find ways to climb out of this black pit. I am telling the story because, although this happened thirty years ago, and in spite of the Women's Movement, women are still getting entrapped in abusive relationships, and returning to them for lack of a sense of self-esteem. And also because of my hard-won knowledge that there is gold to be mined from such shameful experiences. It is a long journey, and requires the confrontation of loving, wise friends, and therapy.

The first thing I needed to do was to get back into my own home, to be on my own ground once more. It wasn't easy for Eleanor to have to move, but a sense of necessity drove me. Then I needed to inform my friends, and I did this by writing and duplicating a very short letter. I don't have a copy, but it was something like this: "I have dissolved a marriage that was no marriage, and returned to the beloved name of Clare Buckland. And I am once again at home on

Camosun Street." Friends were supportive. I remember Mary Rupp honoring the decisiveness of the break with Alex; as a social worker she knew well the stories of women who "loved too much" and gave themselves away forever.

The person who helped me to break the cycle of self-blame was Dr. Howard Thurman. He was a magnificent black philosopher-writer-minister who for years spoke at Canadian Memorial Church at the end of August. I have been so fortunate in my friends! When I was SCM secretary in Toronto, Howard Thurman spent a week in residence on the campus, and when I lived in California I spent a number of hours with him. That summer of 1967 he came to my home for breakfast, and I poured out the story, full of remorse and shame. Howard listened with his open heart, and then said gently: "But you are not God."

The inability to forgive myself for a shameful experience was rooted in the old, old feeling that I ought to be perfect. In spite of my studies of The Records and the reinterpretation of the injunction to "be ye therefore perfect even as your father in heaven is perfect"[3] I had not internalized the better understanding. There is a crucial distinction. The Hebrew and Greek versions of the English translation "perfect" include the ideas of "totality...wholeness...all-inclusiveness." "God makes his sun to rise on the evil *and* on the good, and sendeth rain on the just *and* on the unjust."[4] It is difficult to acknowledge that evil as well as good resides in our psyche. Jungian studies later helped me to come to terms with this unpalatable fact.

For me, having experienced a good deal of success and affirmation, my obsessive sense of shame was an indication of inflation. This upright, intelligent woman should do better than that! Howard reminded me that I am human, with a capacity for stupidity, lack of courage, and plain foolishness. Also with a need for love so great that I could be blind in order to retain a partner.

The next confrontation came later that fall. My position in President McDonald's office came to an abrupt end when he resigned, and Dean Gage offered me either severance pay or a graduate fellowship. I seized the chance to begin a doctoral program, and was admitted as an "unclassified" student in a provisional year. I signed up for as many fourth year psychology courses as were available, including

---

[3] *The Gospel of Matthew*, Chapter 5, verse 48.
[4] *Ibid.* verse 45.

one on Psychopathology. There, for the first time, I discovered the profile of the psychopath, or sociopath, and recognized Alex in every detail: charming, talented, persuasive, superficial, evasive, lying, exploitive...the whole gamut of behaviors that riddle our society and often escape prison. The negatives are hidden from the naive eye behind the charm and shrewdness. I quote Dr. Adolf Guggenbuhl-Craig, a Jungian analyst:

> Decidedly charming, many psychopaths have the facility to flatter and please with grace and elegance. Because Eros does not clutter their relationships, they can dig into their bag of tricks without any inhibitions or scruples. They know, whether consciously or unconsciously, what pleases and flatters. Since love and morality do not get in their way, they often succeed in utterly bewitching those around them.[5]

I also registered for a course with Dr. Ernest Fiedler in the Education faculty because it included study of the new T-Group (Training Group) or Sensitivity Training, movement. I was intrigued by the idea of group process, a whole new field. In the first group experience a man said to me one day: "You are too good to be true". Specifically, I smiled all the time, was always friendly, always helpful, always thoughtful of others, ready to listen — not usually ready to volunteer, seldom angry, and never confrontive! Well, I had to admit it was true. And it was those very qualities, ad nauseam, that I had shown in the relationship with Alex. Unaware. Someone has to be kind enough to tell you such things.

Not being able to put together the kind of doctoral program I wanted, I applied to UCLA to do a program in adult education and behavioral sciences. The major professor was Dr. Paul Sheats, who had studied at the National Training Laboratories where T-Groups were invented, and had founded a western branch at Lake Arrowhead. Also, he encouraged all his students to do as many courses as possible in the Graduate School of Management, which at that time had some core professors who were friends of Abraham Maslow and Carl Rogers. It was a rich environment. Moreover, there were many

---

[5]Adolph Guggenbuhl-Craig: *Eros on Crutches: Reflections on Amorality and Psychopathy.* Spring Publications, University of Dallas, Irving, Texas, 1980, p. 101.

off-campus opportunities for personal growth, and I was still smarting from the Alex affair.

My first venture was to attend a twenty-four hour marathon with a veteran social worker. As we went round the group making our introductions, I said I had been betrayed by a man... The leader immediately cut in: "You mean that you betrayed yourself!" She then made me go around the circle of twelve people and say to each one, "I betrayed myself." That was an about-face which was a turning point, a nodal point in my evolution as a *conscious* person.

I had to examine how it was that I had become so blind that I would consider a relationship so empty of value, so superficial. I had once asked one of Fred's sisters if she could understand that I loved Fred so much that I couldn't face life fully without him. Her nod was reassuring; she had understood. That I had not given myself time to grieve was in part typical of attitudes thirty years ago. People were admired for picking up the pieces and moving on. We didn't know that a year or more is necessary for recovering from a great loss, with no major decisions made. I was in shock from the trauma of death by suicide, even though I had known that Fred was suicidal. I had shut down emotional release in order to block the pain; my perceptions were less acute. I also blocked the data of my senses and my intuition, and my thinking capacity was warped. The marriage with Alex was like a drug, anaesthetizing the pain. In addition, I was working in a church, in an environment where a spiritual approach to tragedy can be a challenge to overcome, to be "strong", in the absence of collective understanding about the grieving process.

These are all valid comments. But the character I had developed that evoked the statement, "You are too good to be true" had to be examined.

A month after the marathon I went to a workshop with Virginia Satir, and on the last night had a nightmare:

> *I was in the basement investigating some pipes that were leaking, when I heard a knock at the front door. There stood two men, Alex and my father. I froze, terrified, and wakened with a splitting headache.*

At breakfast Virginia invited me to work with the dream in the morning session. I waited until the last moment, afraid, and she encouraged me to move into the center and share the dream. I can still experience the trembling, my teeth chattering, as I tried to relive the nightmare. I could hardly get the words out. Virginia coached, asking what were the characteristics of each man, and what did they have in common? It was difficult to see why these two were connected — my father like Alex? Finally it seemed clear that it was a matter of persona. Both were charming men; Alex living behind a front of hard luck; my father behind a front of success. What Alex hid was the truth of his lifestyle. What my father hid was his own impoverished emotional life, cut off from sexuality. Alex relied on my energies, psychic and financial — the dependence of what Guggenbuhl-Craig calls the "emotional invalid". My father, I think quite unconsciously, drew sustenance from his daughter's femininity in lieu of a normal erotic relationship with his wife. Years later, in analysis with Marion Woodman[6], I came to understand this as "psychic incest".

The work with a dream cannot stop with understanding the dream characters. The final task is to ask: how are these qualities embodied in me, and then projected onto others? As I struggled with this, I got severe stomach cramps and doubled up with pain, crying. That much somatic reaction points to a very deep unconscious problem — what Jung termed a "complex", a cluster of experiences around some childhood issue. Because I idealized my father without being close to him through sharing ideas or feelings, I internalized his values and strove always to please him. I developed the characteristics that led to the false persona[7], the covering up of anything deemed negative or inadequate. Indeed, I remember once defining my goal as "to be adequate to any situation". What an impossible, unreal goal! No wonder I find it hard to ask for help, and take such pleasure in being helpful to others. And no wonder my doctoral studies focused on family relationships.

When the dream seemed resolved I felt a great relaxation. Virginia pushed me one step further. She asked me to relax my hips and *move* them! and walk around the circle. It was apparent that I was wearing a tight girdle under my slacks — not uncommon thirty years ago, but less so in California, and especially with pants. My uptight emotional life manifested in an uptight body. Remember age twelve and

---

[6]Author of many books, of which the best known are *Addiction to Perfection* (1982), *The Pregnant Virgin* (1985), and *The Ravaged Bridegroom* (1990), all published by Inner City Books, Toronto, Ontario.

[7]See Glossary.

Cousin Girlie criticizing young women whose breasts visibly wobbled! Amid much laughter I allowed myself to "hang loose", and enjoyed it for the first time. I was fifty-four.

These two experiences, the marathon and the workshop, began an inner revolution that went on reverberating all through my three years at U.C.L.A. Intermittently I raged at Alex, re-doing the scenes where I had remained silent or failed to question. In those moments I was still externalizing the inner pattern, but I was slowly changing my behavior, and forgiving my foolishness. Healing requires both insight and self-compassion. Only then could I *consciously* redeem the self-betrayal. Today there are many more resources in the rich literature about women's lives. The final chapter of *Women Who Run With the Wolves*[8] is especially helpful to women who have made a "poor bargain".

> When the fathering function of the psyche fails to have knowing about issues of soul, we are easily betrayed. (p.395)...The poor bargain she had made was to never say no in order to be consistently loved. (p.398)
>
> In Jungian terms...the antidote [to the complex] is consciousness of one's foibles and gifts, so that the complex is unable to act on its own. (p.438)

Today, Chaos theory has helped me to understand the complex process involved in a major life shift. I found affirmation recently in an insightful article by Frederick David Abraham entitled "Chaos, Courage, Choice, and Creativity"[9].

In the catastrophe of the Alex episode I had experienced *psychic* chaos, and multiple forces interacted to force me to choose either regression or individuation. My work with Jung and the Records study gave me the courage to be open to new learning and to make that major shift in behavior — a shift toward a more creative life pattern.

It may seem strange that I am moved to quote Chaos theory. Even all these years later, I was excited to find a scientific parallel for the struggle I had endured to move from the hell of psychic chaos toward a new life. Later, I turned to quantum physics for understand-

[8]Clarissa Pinkola-Estés: *Women Who Run With the Wolves*. N.Y. Ballantine Books, 1992.
[9]Frederick David Abraham: "Chaos, Courage, Choice, & Creativity", p.66 in *Psychological Perspectives,* op.cit., Issue 31, 1995.

ing of *religious* experience. My mind always seems to search for validation of feeling or intuitive insight in intellectual terms. Having grown up in a "sensible", black-or-white family, and in a rational culture, I have found it hard to trust non-rational or irrational experience.

The shifting of my "pattern", of my "ground plan" of needing to be loved, and of despair over being alone in the world and without a partner, required depth psychology to assist the re-organization of that focus. What I am grateful for in this whole dark experience is the discovery of a different kind of strength, more self-aware, more discriminating. I doubt that anything less extreme in the way of a "lesson" could have penetrated the barrier of my socialization experience. More work had to be done later in Jungian analysis to help me see how the "father's daughter" role affected all my relationships with men. But I had learned enough in 1968 to redeem a sense of myself and point in new directions for personal growth. Gold had been found in the dark minefields of self-betrayal.

8
A New Path Opens

Fate has a bright face as well as a dark one, an understanding I was able to reach only through suffering. That I was able to attend the University of California at Los Angeles for a doctoral program was a true gift that rested on the falling apart of earlier plans.

The position in the President's office at U.B.C. held no future, and it collapsed when President MacDonald resigned. Because of that cancelled contract I was given a grant for graduate study, and having been out of school for thirty years I had to enroll in a provisonal program to qualify for doctoral studies. I wanted to pursue a program that would help me create new ways of approaching family education, but in the end this proved to be impossible at U.B.C. Yet it was Professor Fiedler, a maverick in the Faculty of Education at that time, who was uniquely able to introduce me to developments in group process, a field of study that was just opening up. Through him I learned of the adult education program at UCLA and the pioneering work of Dr. Paul Sheats.

In November of that year, 1967, I flew down to UCLA to explore possibilities for study, and after two or three introductions I met LuAnn Darling in the Personnel Department, who was herself mapping out a special program in Adult Education with Paul Sheats. That chance meeting led not only to collaboration on our dissertations, but to our lasting friendship.

Financing the studies was another question that got answered by a series of miracles. A friend from Branksome Hall, Mary McLean, was head of the McLean Foundation, and I applied to them — unsuccessfully, because my proposal was too full of educational jargon for a lay committee to tolerate. But Mary gave me a personal grant of a thousand dollars. Once established as a student, I applied to the American Association of University Women for one of their international fellowships, and won enough money to fund a three-year doctoral program. I could hardly believe my good fortune. The connection with that body held many pleasures as I reported at their annual meetings my excitement in the development of new ideas, and was affirmed by their enthusiasm.

Still another connection opened new opportunities. Dr. Larry Erickson, Dean of Graduate Studies, invited me to his office to offer congratulations on the fellowship, and invited me to do some work for him as a research assistant. His field was further education for high school teachers of commerce; and my association with him led to summer school work each year through graduation and beyond. I coordinated his program, did an occasional lecture, and was paid handsomely, even acquiring the title of Assistant Professor. The only altercation we had occurred when he used some material I had written without acknowledgement — an all-too-frequent practice in graduate schools. This was after I had finished my degree, and I confronted him in the hall, furious. He defended himself on the grounds that this was customary with graduate students, to which I replied: "I am no longer your student; I am a colleague now!" He apologized. In spite of this we continued to be good friends when I returned for a post-doctoral year in 1972.

I wanted more than friendship, but that was not to be, and appropriately so. A beneficent Fate has saved me from many a false step, each time with new learning purchased at a cost. A "father's daughter" has a lot to learn about relationships with men. Journal notes and dreams from that period paint the picture.

> I was aware that Larry responded to my values, but that he seemed to be without spiritual grounding...to want meaning in his life but without enough development of consciousness to know how to move, or to be ready to commit himself to the search...a man caught in a transitional confusion. I saw that I had become threatening to him because I was so open that he backed off... He may have a *healthy* fear of my apparent willingness to take

charge of his growth! His very stubborn "loner" kind of strength says, "Let me get out of this myself!"

So here were my energies for growth focused on a strong but wounded man, wanting to be involved in his healing, pushing him to choose to be healed, not really honoring what I knew intellectually, that "That is his choice." I admired him enormously, was valued as a colleague, but in the personal woman-to-man realm was unable to connect freely around feelings or to elicit comment.

During those years, a professor in a seminar related to sensitivity training had said to me: "I see you as a person well able to be supportive, but not to confront." Just as with my father, I found it almost impossible to speak of feelings once I had put a man on a pedestal.

I had a long struggle with this split between thinking and feeling. During all my sixty years and until I was in training to become a Jungian analyst, I had assumed that my dominant function was *thinking*. I had developed it early and well, and it served me well in the professional world. It had also become highly developed in the doctoral program.

There was another problem, that of "mothering", which can be a hazard of the "helpful" attitude. Two dreams recorded in this period shocked me into facing this aspect of my relationships with men.

> *It is early in the morning, and I am packing my suitcase to leave, when mother comes in to me and says that she is to go into hospital for further surgery...that the cancer has returned, and that she is facing the fact that she may not come through this time. I waken, sad. The immediate thought comes: "Mothering is disease; sexuality is health", and I connect it to the fantasy that I am "taking care of Larry's need" in a neurotic kind of mothering.*
>
> *I sleep, and dream again of packing, sorting, discarding... I come upon two pairs of underpants belonging to my son. I give them to him, and say good-bye. I tell him: "I dreamed of you last night, and realized that mothering is not a good thing for me to do, and that I am glad to be reminded of your own happy sexuality. This is what I have learned in relation to Larry." My son smiles and agrees... Half awake again, I*

have the additional thought that mothering is something one outgrows as one gets older and there is no need for it. It becomes cancerous if not discarded.

Still another dream, of buying more than I want from a baker woman, and getting dry rusks that I didn't want, taught me that helpfulness not requested, and proffered out of longing for relationship, exacts a high price. The friendship is distorted, and rejection hurts. Again, I looked at what had happened with my father. I bought his masculine values, including the "shoulds" and the driving force toward achievement, at the cost of my autonomy as a loved child to grow in my own way. What I got, side by side with the real achievement, was in some ways dry bread, rusks, the life gone out of the bread of life, the feminine principle of relatedness damaged.

The healing of that particular relationship with Larry was completed in an Intensive Journal workshop.[1] There I used active imagination to write a dialogue with Larry in which each of us expressed the feelings and insights that had never been shared. One connection became clear: I wrote: "I am aware of your hands — they are my father's hands, as mine are..." Ten years later, in analysis with Marion Woodman, I realized that Larry *was* the idealized father with the wounded feminine side, and that I wanted his love of me as a woman. I wanted to be allowed to participate in the healing of the split in him so that I might heal my own. Both of us had lost some of the connection with the Self as children.

Shortly after writing this chapter, I dreamed of Larry — a different Larry :

> *He looks in my eyes, and says: "You are the most beautiful woman I know" — to which I do not respond. He is helping me lay pieces of wood around the foundation of the house; they seem to serve some special purpose. I am aware that he is grieving for someone who has died, and am conscious of what a sweet, generous person he is, older, more mature, calmer. Later I realize how he has changed, and say to him: "Larry, I wish I were fifteen years younger!" and he embraces me. Stacking silver flatware in the dishwasher — my mother's silver — I recognize how much I love him...*

---

[1]Ira Progoff: *At a Journal Workshop*. New York, Dialogue House Library, 1975.

Awake, I become aware of how time is not linear, and each of us has been transformed in the more than twenty years since I was at U.C.L.A.

* * * * *

Parallel to the personal learning was the enormous intellectual excitement that U.C.L.A. offered. As I recall the research and writing of the dissertation, I relive the mounting delight in bringing together diverse resources for family education, and a wholly new sense of a disciplined research theory — an aspect I would never have thought I could relish! The purpose of the whole endeavor was to develop a model, a theory, of effective parent education in an increasingly stressful society.

In that environment I became aware of many new developments which could contribute to parent education, and I did intensive investigation of six areas. These included family group therapy, the system concept and family interaction; small group research — decision-making, leadership and power; organization development and team building; laboratory training and experiential learning; psychotherapeutic process — the helping relationship; and creativity research — the characteristics and conditions of creativity. What a rich mining of ideas! All these areas contributed ideas for teaching and processes for work with a single family group, or a group of three or four families together. I titled the dissertation: "Toward a Theory of Parent Education: A Comparative Qualitative Analysis of Learning Models". The very academic summary statement reads:

A theoretical model for parent education is presented in system terms, offering criteria of excellence in developing programs beamed at families as open human systems. The study is qualitative and analytical, building a preliminary model by induction from data from literature and the field, then by deduction formulating propositions and hypotheses for empirical testing. Behavioral objectives and learning processes are derived from examination of the behavioral sciences to determine (1) future relevant characteristics suitable for socialization goals in the post-industrial society, and (2) facilitative strategies for fur-

thering such valued behaviors. The orientation is human-
istic, and the sample population broadly middle class.

It's clear that I had used (over-used) my thinking function! But
the process was utterly satisfying in its challenge and at graduation
earned me the added magic words "With Distinction".

Apart from researching the literature I did "participant observation" in existing programs — which was interesting in itself. For instance, I explored George Bach's "fight training" groups and there I
learned to confront! One particular workshop design was to divide
men and women into two groups in separate rooms, and require participants, one at a time, to go to the other-sex group and express feelings about relationships. Petrified, I hung back, but began to
smoulder as every single man did nothing but complain about how
women treated him. By the time my turn came I was so angry that I
stormed into the men's group and without any hesitation told them:
"I'm fed up with your belly-aching! Why don't you look at your
own behavior?" There was a stunned silence, and Dr. Bach said,
"You know, she's right." But there were other times when one-to-
one confrontation was still difficult. I wanted to be liked.

Studying group process meant participating in a group program
called "Leadership Development" over in the Graduate School of
Management — a year-long experience in the one-way vision laboratory. It was a tremendous personal learning experience under the
tutelage of Professor Arthur Shedlin, to whom I paid tribute in my
dissertation as one "who by precept and by modeling taught me to
trust the creative process in me and to taste its delights."

As I worked with the new "grounded theory" model of Glaser
and Strauss[2] which enabled me to bypass statistical experimental research, I became more and more excited by the possibility of developing an evolving theory which could be field-tested. Using my
mind in a disciplined and complex study was exhilarating, and
when I graduated in 1971 I was feeling competent and happy in my
chosen field. Later, in Vancouver in 1973, I was able to use some of
the ideas in the first Family Place experiment on the west side.

---

[2]B.G.Glaser and A.L.Strauss: *The Discovery of Grounded Theory: Strategies for Qualitative Research.*Chicago, Aldine Publishing Co., 1967.

In my files I've come across a poem written at New Year's 1971, at Four Springs in California. It captures the sense of exhilaration I was experiencing during those years at U.C.L.A. I titled it "The Feast".

Oh that beautiful new sense of joy
Singing in me!
Interior joy, nameless, unaccountable,
But saying Yes! to crisp air,
Wood smoke, cold water,
The song of the rain, the friend's touch.
Yes! to the young Child out there,
And in me, to all the emerging possibilities of being
    creative.
My heart leaps, I catch my breath —
To love life SO MUCH!
And to know, too, that this is a joy
That cannot be taken from me by loss of a loved one.
It simply is, born of pain, of difficult choices,
Of commitment to choose always the better way.
And out of this feast,
The abundant joy in learning, loving, living at the
    growing edge.
Life, I thank you!
I said Yes to the darkness too long and was trapped in it,
Preoccupied with assimilating pain, facing weakness,
    exploring tears.
It became for me a defense
Against affirming my creativity, acting on it, believing I
    could...
Trusting the alarming possibility of being able.
When I acted on that premise,
Said Yes to the new demand to create,
Then joy came to dwell with me.

The next day I learned that my father had died. All the previous fall he had been in a coma following a severe stroke. I had been at home in Vancouver doing a semester of research, and had seen him a few times, unsure whether he had recognized me. Christmas came and went, and I was scheduled to return to campus. There was a slight change for the worse in his condition, and I was in a dilemma about "waiting for him to die". I finally decided to leave, and telephoned daily as I drove south, heading for a retreat at Four Springs where I wanted to be with my father in spirit, meditatively, in my own way. In retrospect, I would now choose to sit with him in hospital, talking to him quietly, hour by hour...but that perspective on the person dying in coma was not then available to me. What I did write, in the long hours alone at Four Springs, was a tribute which I like to think his consciousness received, a tuning in to the bond between us. I placed in the fire, to be transformed, a dead pine cone which seemed to symbolize a form which life had vacated. Its surfaces were spongy, shrunken, its seeds gone, even though the shape was there. The pine cone will yield to the natural dying-process which is part of life; it will become the humus for new forest growth. And I wrote a farewell:

> As a pebble dropped in a pool
> So was I born...and the ripples spread
> And multiplied; and sun and rain and storm
> Were over me...and then he who was my father
> Was taken home, and the bell tolled....
> It tolls for thee, for me, and I honor his name.

It feels extraordinary, now, that I wrote the poem celebrating Life in that same weekend. My father had shared my struggles, and I hope he knew and shared the newfound joy.

There is one other piece to the story of my father's death. I chose not to fly home for the private memorial service, partly because my car was packed with all my possessions and hard to leave safely, but mostly because I was so alienated from my stepmother that I felt I would contribute nothing to her and that the mourning had been happening for all the preceding months. I wish now that I had gone home and been present. She felt that I was hard-hearted. And years later, when I had grown close to Auntie Grace, the sister who adored him, I realized that she longed to have me accompany her to Victoria, and share the sorrow. I had wrestled with my feelings, but was not conscious enough to embrace the whole picture.

* * * * *

When I first returned home after graduation Vancouver seemed like a flatland in contrast to the stimulation of U.C.L.A. and the excitement of what I had learned. Someone suggested this was a typical post-doctoral depression, and it certainly *felt* like that! In spite of the fact that I had been able to arrange a year of substitute teaching in the School of Home Economics, on my favorite subject of communication, I did not enjoy that post. I think teaching requires more of a sense of drama than I have, more extraversion. The one bright light in that desert year was Pat Thom, the program director in the Center for Continuing Education. She was pioneering a course called Options for Women, the beginning of what was to become the Women's Resource Center, and she invited me to plan a lecture-discussion series. The Women's Movement was just beginning in Vancouver, and the women who enrolled in that course were hungry for new ideas and skills for their personal growth. I loved the work.

Had there been the possibility of full-time employment I probably would have been content to work for the Center. Instead, my longing for the atmosphere of U.C.L.A. and my friends there led to a decision to apply for a post-doctoral fellowship, and I returned to California. Not that I was sure this was a right move; but after much weighing of the issues, in gestalt fashion, feeling held the upper hand, and I sold my house and shipped everything I wanted to keep to Los Angeles. Sometimes I have regretted letting go of the lovely home on Camosun Street without even consulting my sons. Previously I had rented it, sometimes with happy results, but the last time disastrously. I had come home to find a puppy had scratched the new screen doors, chewed a hole in a Navajo rug, and demolished handles on Indian baskets inherited from my mother. But I could have continued to rent it, and there would have been a place for all of us to call "home".

Some of the pull was the deep connection with friends, who had been another source of joy in those years at U.C.L.A. LuAnn Darling was no longer on staff there, but we renewed our connection and gradually became close friends. Their home was a "home away from home" for me, and as her own doctoral plans progressed we found ourselves using the same theoretical systems approach, she in the field of organizational development and I with family education. Patricia Baker was doing a degree in Behavioral Science, and we shared the lab experience in group process. All three of us consulted and shared ideas, and LuAnn helped with typing my thesis. When the time came for assembling the huge tome, all three of us worked on the floor of my little apartment, the laughter countering my exhaustion. Sometimes Jackie Schwartz joined us, and I became part of her family also, linked by a shared affection for Virginia Satir.

These were friendships with a strong intellectual component as well as affection. When I returned in 1972 for the post-doctoral year on campus, Pat greeted me with Castaneda's first book on his encounters with the shaman Don Juan, opening a new door in my thinking. LuAnn and Pat and I brainstormed a design for a workshop on creativity which we carried out the following October.

My friendship with Pat had, and continues to have, a very special quality. She continued her studies in the Graduate School of Management and then after ten years consulting in two giant corporations, frustrated with their policies and attitudes, returned to school to train as a therapist. She chose the Institute of Transpersonal Psychology in Menlo Park, earned her doctorate, and became a licensed psychologist — no mean feat for a woman in her late fifties. Like me, she has worked in depth in her own therapy, and shares a spiritual search. In introducing me to the world of Don Juan, she initiated my continuing exploration to understand our perceptions of "reality". Pat has recently bought land on Lopez Island in the San Juans, and I look forward to summer visits.

Later Jean Renshaw joined our three-some, a much younger woman who had earned her Ph.D. in the Graduate School of Management and gone on to teaching and consulting, and later, on a Fullbright Fellowship, to researching the changing situation of women in Japan and Korea. Jean and LuAnn and Pat and I have had many wonderful reunions at LuAnn's home, marked always by a visit to our favorite bookstore and a Mexican dinner, complete with margaritas. LuAnn is currently writing a book on mentoring, and I was one of her two hundred or more people to be interviewed about our own experiences of mentoring. We are all four different temperamentally, making for rich, stimulating sharing.

In these years the friendship with Hedy Holt, my Lanz friend, became closer and many times I stayed in their home while hunting for still another bachelor apartment. Each summer between semesters at U.C.L.A. I had gone home, all my worldly goods packed in my convertible; and each fall I packed them up again to return and create a new "home". Over those years I met friends of the Darlings, Felicia and Leon Papernow, and enjoyed the luscious bouquets of orchids from her garden. Later, when I flew to San Francisco for a Jungian workshop, she and Leon drove up to take me out for lunch and walk along the waterfront. Felicia was a dancer and is a fine painter, and she, too, is very dear. I have spent many memorable times in their beautiful home in Santa Cruz, the last two overshadowed by sorrow. On my way to a Tibetan retreat on Death and Dying I spent three days there saying "good-bye" to Leon, who was terminally ill, and six months later spent time with a grieving Felicia.

The post-doctoral year was a luxury. Its status allowed me to have a student medical card, to be an associate of the Faculty Club, and to audit any classes my heart desired, with the consent of the instructor. Hungry for new experiences, I got permission to enroll in a seminar with one of my former professors in consultation process, a class in clay sculpture and one in dance therapy. I loved working in clay, but having attempted to model the head of my friend Pat Baker without prior experience in anatomy or three-dimensional drawing the result was frustrating. And in dance therapy I felt like an aging clown in the class of young dancers. It was good learning, sometimes painful, and the reading on imagination was stimulating.

Another door opened professionally. I met a woman in the Extension Department who invited me to coordinate a new program in training lay counselors for adults, and in the spring I accepted the offer to teach the course on Aging. What a challenge! In the same spirit that led me to accept the principalship of York House without ever having taught school, I assumed that I could learn what I needed to know about age. It was hard work, and rewarding. The field of gerontology was opening up, and there were many new books by the leading figures of that period and fascinating research studies from the National Institute of Mental Health.

Encouraged by this new development, I applied for the position of director of adult education in U.C.L.A.' s enormous extension department. Clearly, I didn't have the experience required for such a job, and it would have killed me had I got it! Fate, or the Self, knows better than the ego what is needed for one's life. By the time June came, I knew in my heart that Vancouver was "home" for me, and I packed up my belongings and shipped everything back.

Without having a job in mind; just "knowing" that was what I had to do.

Nevertheless, all of these experiences have linked me to the United States by ties of affection. When my sons were of school age I had become an American citizen; but when Morgan and I were divorced and I returned to Canada I regained my Canadian citizenship. I still feel connected by many bonds to the land where my studies were so fruitful and friendships so warm. There are now other links with American colleagues through Jungian Analysts • North Pacific, and I travel back and forth to meetings, thankful for the Pace program which allows me to bypass the border line-ups. The story of that organization belongs to still another era of my long life.

9

THE LONG JOURNEY TO TRUE VOCATION

... each of us is who we are because of the contributions of many other people and beings with whom
our lives have intersected. They have contributed to
the overall pattern that we call ourselves. We are
bundles of crossroads, each one a point at which
some new or unexplored or unexpected aspect of
ourselves emerged and became incorporated into
our sense of ourselves.

David Spangler[1]

Timing is such an amazing fact of our lives. When I had returned
to Vancouver in 1971, no doors opened. When I came back in 1973,
the whole world seemed to welcome me.

The west side of Vancouver was flourishing: housing vacancies
were 0.03% and there was a strike on elevator construction. I had to
wait almost three months to occupy a new apartment block, Chancel-
lor Court, adjacent to U.B.C. — one well worth waiting for. I was
staying with my friends Theresa and Ralph Spitzer, and when walking one evening as the sunset across Burrard Inlet and the mountains
was spectacular, we had climbed to the seventh floor of this new
building, and I knew that was where I wanted to live. Where to stay

---

[1]David Spangler: "The Cosmic Christ", p.144 in David Spangler and
William I. Thompson: *Reimagination of the World*. Santa Fe, N.M., Bear &
Co., 1991.

meanwhile? Virginia and Jack Mackay had a guest bedroom and invited me to stay as long as I needed a space. She had been one of the Founders and an art teacher at York House, and had known me from high school days, so it was a happy arrangement, an auspicious beginning to a new era.

I had returned without knowing what work I would find. All I knew was that I wanted an opportunity to develop in practice the creative ideas about family education that my doctoral studies had birthed. My thesis contended that "parent" education would be most fruitful if it were "family" education, as found in the Danish family learning centers. These I had read about while at U.C.L.A., as a type of community center where there were educational programs for all members of families, singly and together. And Lo and Behold! a little store-front operation called "Family Place" had begun to operate on the west side of Vancouver, funded by one of the New Democratic Party experimental Local Initiative Projects.

Its founding is an interesting story. Ellen LeFevre and a friend had gone to a ten-year high school reunion and discovered that most of the young mothers were isolated and lonely in the suburbs, finding no way to share their parenting struggles. So these two young mothers obtained a grant and rented a store-front with space for a playroom, an office, and a large sitting room area where the mothers could talk while their toddlers were supervised. The Model served a crucial need, and has survived to be duplicated in a number of areas in the Greater Vancouver area. Now, in September, they were looking for a coordinator at a salary of four hundred dollars a month.

I applied for the position, and went for an interview with their Board of Directors. The chairman, Dr. Alan Cashmore, a child and family psychiatrist, listened to my ideas about a family learning center, and asked: "How is it that having just finished a doctoral program you are willing to work for four hundred dollars a month?" Good question. My enthusiasm for bringing my dream to life, building on the dreaming that created Family Place, carried the night, and I was hired. I gave Dr. Cashmore a copy of the published article based on my dissertation, and he came to spend an evening with me. That was the beginning of a deepening friendship, treasured until his untimely death from leukemia on March 28, 1992.

Alan was an Englishman, small in stature with a crown of red gold curly hair and a beard, always seen with a pipe and a twinkle in his blue eyes. He had trained as a child and family psychiatrist in London,

Alan Cashmore

and had come to Canada originally with his eight-year-old son, Peter, to apply for a position as Director of the newly formed Children's Foundation. In the end, he joined the Greater Vancouver Mental Health Association and was one of the founders of Blenheim House, a treatment center for preschool children and their parents. He came to be a person honored for his struggles on behalf of children's well-being, and when Blenheim House finally moves to its new home it will be re-named Cashmore House. One of my loved possessions is a

125

portrait of Alan, given to me by his wife, Kay, after his death. It captures Alan's serious, reflective quality in its warm brown tones, pipe in hand, looking directly at me in my living room.

The riches of our sharing are part of the fabric of my being, and I miss him sorely. I think the best way to convey this is to include here what my heart wrote for his memorial service.

> I want to celebrate Alan's gift for friendship, which is the way I knew him best. We began as colleagues, working together at Family Place, and co-leading groups for foster parents and nurses. Gradually the friendship deepened, and we were just two people who needed and loved to talk with each other. For eighteen years we had a standing date for lunch, every week, usually at my place — an hour or so between work assignments of sharing talk about anything that was on our minds or hearts that week. This was one of the richest experiences of my life.
>
> Both of us had learned about communication from Virginia Satir, and what was so marvellous was that we could practise being "real" with each other. There was no place or need for "making" conversation. The pace was slow, as you might expect from two introverts — there were lots of pauses, and silence was comfortable. From Alan I learned what it is to be "present". He was always right *there*. He listened with all of himself, and by look or phrase showed that he had "heard". Often he "heard" what I hadn't yet brought to consciousness — and then we could share a new thought, or a new feeling. We tried to *stay with feelings*, even when that was hard, and in those eighteen years there were rough places as well as celebrations. We helped each other to stay connected.
>
> Therapists learn to do this with patients or clients, but I think it is a rare gift between equals, and especially, perhaps, between a man and a woman where there is no sexual relationship involved. It was a gift we both treasured.
>
> When Alan was in remission from the chemotherapy, and we had to face together what was so inevitable, I wanted to be sure that he *knew* how loved he was and what his life had contributed to so many people. So I read him something that had touched me. It is a quotation

from Dostoyevsky, followed by a fragment of a poem by Raymond Carver:[2]

> Without suffering, happiness cannot be
>   understood.
> The ideal passes through suffering
>   like gold through fire
> And did you get what you wanted from this life,
>   even so?
> I did.
> And what did you want?
> To call myself beloved, to feel myself
> beloved on the earth.

Alan was quiet awhile, and then nodded, and said "Yes, I think I do." I felt glad — and we can all be glad that he finally was able to receive the tributes, the love from so many directions. In the desolate days this week as I searched for a phrase that would speak to grief, I came upon lines from The Prophet[3] with which I will close:

> For what is it to die but to stand naked in the
>   wind and to melt into the sun?
> And what is it to cease breathing but to free the
>   breath
> from life's restless tides, that it may rise and
>   expand
> and seek God unencumbered?

I think that is how it is with Alan now.

Alan was mentor as well as friend. After I had moved from the Coordinator position into offering to consult with families sitting together informally on the floor at Family Place; and when funding could no longer support a staff person exclusively for that work, Alan asked one day: "Why don't you acknowledge that you are, in fact, a "therapist", not just a consultant? And go into private practice?" I stalled for awhile. My degree was in adult education and behavioral sciences, not in psychology, and I considered myself an

---

[2]Cited in Linda Leonard: *Witness to the Fire*, frontispiece. Boston, Shambala, 1989.

[3]Kahlil Gibran: *The Prophet*. London, William Heinemann Ltd., 1926.

"educator". It felt presumptuous to call myself a "therapist", and even risky. But Alan prevailed, and finally I drafted an announcement, reading: CLARE BUCKLAND has opened a private practice as Individual and Family Group Consultant. [sic!] And inside the folded card, after listing my degree, I note that

> all of her study was oriented toward family education and consultation, and work with groups. Non-academic learning experiences include Jungian analysis, extensive workshop experience in a variety of psychological approaches, and family therapy training with Virginia Satir and David Freeman.
>
> In her work with individuals, couples, families and groups Dr. Buckland uses a consultative approach stemming from a firm conviction that human beings have many resources for solving their own problems in living.
>
> With assistance in looking at behavior that is self-defeating, in clarifying what they wish to change, and learning more effective ways of communicating, most people can reduce stress and achieve a more fulfilling life.
>
> Family groups, including children, are encouraged to study the way their family works and to develop new ways of relating which are more satisfying for each family member.
>
> The fee, whether individual or family, is $25.00 per session of approximately one hour.

Clearly, this is an educational approach to "problems in living". My journal records that even at the time I was wondering how long that approach would continue to be representative of *me*. The shift toward working more with clues from the unconscious realm came gradually, and happened with the surprising discovery that my greatest enjoyment came from working with clients who brought dreams to our sessions. My love of Jung, and my own work with journalling and dreams, surfaced in new ways. All through the years I had continued to read Jungian books — mostly books written by people trained by Jung — and that had always been my source of nourishment and inspiration. Eventually, I *felt* like a "therapist"! And eventually, I decided to undergo Jungian training — but that is another story.

While at Family Place I met Lilly Jaffe, an art therapist, and the two of us decided to buy a house which could be shared by two other people, a project that had long been part of a fantasy of cooperative living. So I packed up my belongings once again, and stored them at the house while I went to Peru to visit Suyin and John Lee who were in Arequipa for a year. I find a journal entry written on December 12, 1975, while awaiting take-off. I have opened a gift from Jacie Boyes, Hanna Bauer's book, *I Came to My Island*,[4] and I write:

> I am aware that I am in/on an "island" of my own, here in the waiting room, feeling rich, and richly loved, richly experiencing, now, here....Virginia's great pleasure in the news of my house keeps washing over me, multiplying my own. She is so excited, so jubilant for me, in a way I didn't expect. What a lovely generosity of spirit to overflow so spontaneously for a friend's experience!... [Virginia, as I said, was the friend with whom I had stayed while waiting for the Chancellor Court apartment.]

The three weeks in Peru provided a varied experience of another culture, the wonderful crafts and silver and costuming and food. We travelled to Cusco and on to Machu Picchu, where we stayed one night in the small lodge right at the site. The early morning was magnificent as the mists gradually rose over the ancient stones, and we could wander without tourists intruding. Suyin's family hiked one of the precipitous trails to a still taller mountain, while I waited peacefully in the sun at what must have been a sundial, gazing out over endless valleys. For my eightieth birthday Suyin had a T-shirt printed with a picture of me seated there. On another occasion Suyin and I journeyed alone to Lake Titicaca on the border between Peru and Bolivia, and once again experienced the market and drove out to other ancient stones overlooking the world from 12,000 feet. I feel so appreciative of the storehouse of images granted by that interlude between moving and work in the world.

Back in Vancouver I moved into our new home — "Highbury House" — in January 1976. It was an interesting house, with the living room upstairs, a view out over the Fraser River delta, and a won-

---

[4]Hanna Bauer: *I Came to My Island: A Journey Through the Experience of Change*. Seattle, WA., B. Straub Publishing Co., 1973.

derful sunny deck where Lilly and I and an occasional guest did yoga. Her bedroom and a study were on that floor, and mine were downstairs, a lovely room with a fireplace which I made into a bed-sitting-room. In my enthusiasm for getting settled I carried too many boxes up those stairs, and ended up with an impaired disk, on my back for five weeks. Lilly and I found two men who wanted to share cooperative living, a plan which was happy at times, but with built-in inequalities in finance and responsibility for chores and the large garden. In the end, I grew desperate for my own private space, and after much negotiation and with mixed feelings we agreed that I would move out. I found an apartment in Kerrisdale, the area in which I had grown up, on the twelfth floor with a spectacular view to the southwest. Alan came to inspect my choice, and we blessed the space together. Auntie Grace gifted me with carpeting, and I furnished the second bedroom as the study where I would work with clients. There I lived happily for nine years.

Parallel to work with individuals, which in private practice can often be a lonely way of life, I began to have a lively and adventurous life in the burgeoning Women's Movement. The Women's Resources Center pioneered groups for women beginning to reach out for new ways to experience autonomy and develop a sense of self-worth. And I plunged wholeheartedly into creating programs. At first I focused on the family, with groups titled: "The Family as a Growth Center", and "Parenting Skills for the New Family", sometimes in cooperation with the Unitarian Church or the School of Social Work where I had studied with Dr. David Freeman a type of family therapy centered around the family of origin. But one program became a core offering over a long period: "Developing Potential for Growth and Change". This was a prototype of the many workshops prompted by the Women's Movement, covering such topics as self-esteem, anger, assertiveness, relationships, communication. Sometimes today a woman will approach me and say, "Years ago I was in one of your Developing Potential groups, and that was a new beginning for me!" After awhile we offered a second level, and then a third which we called "Encountering Yourself"; and still another on "Knowing Yourself Through Dreams".

A large part of my pleasure in all of this work was the sense of being part of a team and working with talented women as co-leaders — people like Jacie Boyes, Joan Hendry, Eileen Hendry, Irene Suyin Lee, and Joyce Frazee. Ruth Sigal and I led a number of groups simply titled, "On Loneliness"; and Bob Boyes and I designed a program of "Life Planning for Men and Women Over 35: Toward a Sense of Meaning".

Some of the exercises for experiential learning became standard handouts, and also became central to my own way of being. One was "Aids for Giving and Receiving Feedback" which originated with Dr. George Lehner, a professor of psychology at U.C.L.A. I wish everyone could experience the wisdom of the suggestions he offers. For instance: "Focus feedback on behavior rather than the person...on observations rather than inferences...on description rather than judgment...on the sharing of ideas and information rather than on giving advice."

Another powerful tool was the "Johari Window", so-named for Joseph Luft and Harry Ingham, two psychologists at U.C.L.A.[5] This is an awareness model of human interaction, a diagram in four quadrants named Open, Blind, Hidden, and Unknown. The first two, at the top, are "Known to Others": the Open area known to self and the Blind area not known to self. The two lower quadrants are not known to others: the Hidden area known to self, however; and the Unknown area literally out of consciousness — behavior, feelings and motivation known neither to self nor to others. I worked with this model in terms of awareness and self-disclosure, and in terms of willingness to change: to be open to feedback, to look at what we hide as sometimes necessary and appropriate and sometimes unnecessary and doing us a disservice. And to allow what is unconscious to surface through dreams and "a purposeful movement toward synthesis, order, balance and growth of a living Center, the Self."

One of the workshop handouts was my own summation which I titled, "The Communication Continuum: Dimensions of Respect for Self and Other". The horizontal dimensions were Avoidance, Superlogic, Non-assertion, Aggression, and Assertion. The vertical categories are questions: How am I taking care of self? How am I caring for other? and How am I taking care of the issue or situation? The spread sheet contains a quotation from Erich Fromm which I have been unable to locate, but which I love: "Respect for one's own integrity, love and understanding of one's own self, cannot be sepa-

---

[5]Joseph Luft: *Of Human Interaction*. Palo Alto, California, National Press Books, 1969, pp.13,14.

rated from respect for and love and understanding of another individual".

One particular exercise, learned sometime around 1976 in a workshop with John Enright, a California psychologist, had significant repercussions in my own life. In these years my Auntie Grace — everyone called her "Auntie Grace" — who had lived in her own apartment to the grand old age of ninety-seven, was now in a private hospital and needing attention from me. She looked forward to going out to dinner every Sunday night, and I was sometimes complaining to myself about this routine. Dr. Enright's exercise asks us to look at the "should" or "have to" situation, and decide what the consequences of *not* taking the action in question would be. I realized that I would feel miserable about myself if I refused to do this act of kindness for someone who loved me and was extraordinarily generous toward me. Miraculously, my attitude shifted: I *chose* to take her to dinner every Sunday night, and never again experienced the grumbling, even when tired. Teaching one of the Developing Potential groups this exercise, I shared my experience, describing Auntie Grace as a remarkable woman with a keen mind who still beat opponents at Scrabble. At the end of the session a young woman introduced herself as Lorraine Waring, and said she would love to play Scrabble with Auntie Grace! That led to regular visits, sometimes taking along her small daughter, Wynne; and later she and her husband, Aubrey, helped with the one hundredth birthday party for this beloved old lady. One never knows what will unfold!

Nor could I foresee how precious that relationship with Auntie Grace would become. As her eyesight and hearing failed, and she was aware of her life drawing to a close, she would often sit in my living room watching the sun set, and reciting lines from her favorite poem: "*Sunset and evening star, and one clear call for me, And may there be no moaning of the bar when I set out to sea.*"[6]

As I grow older myself she is often in my mind, helping me to accept increasing limitations of physical strength, and to be thankful for aliveness of mind and feeling. Her generosity also made more possible the owning of my own home, first with the gift toward the purchase of the Camosun house, and later, after her death, the pur-

---

[6]Alfred Lord Tennyson: "Crossing the Bar" in *The Norton Anthology of English Literature*, Fourth Edition, Vol.2. New York, W.W. Norton & Company, 1962, p. 1216.

chase of the beautiful condominium at The Lagoons. In addition, it would have been much more difficult to finance the costly Jungian training without the inheritance from Auntie Grace. Those funds have always been considered a family trust, helping, for instance, to purchase university scholarship funds for grandchildren, and enabling me, I hope, to leave at least part of the value of my home to the next generations.

As I became more involved with the Jungian training I had to let go of the work with groups. I missed it, missed the wonderful people involved in those programs and the teamwork with the Volunteer Associates. When the Women's Resources Center celebrated their ten year "Decade of Change", they invited me to participate in the panel of speakers. This is what I shared:

> There is a very special kind of happiness in being with all of you tonight, and invited to say something about commitment to being a whole person. I've missed being an active part of the team at the Center, and every few months Anne Ironside and I meet to share what's been happening with us as women, and in our work in the world. When we talked last May, she asked if I would be willing to share a dream...and I agreed.
>
> In the ten years when I was involved with many of you in workshops on personal growth, we worked — as was appropriate — on feeling better about ourselves, more hopeful, more skillful, more assertive in developing our potential. And then I grew older...and (as was appropriate) I turned more and more to the inner life, and began to study Jung more closely, and to train as a Jungian analyst. That training involves personal work in depth, and I learned how my focus on achievement in my father's style had led me away from my own feminine self...And then slowly a new relationship to the masculine began, and revealed itself in dreams, in what I experience as an "inner marriage". It is one of these dreams I want to share.
>
> *It is evening. I go into a jewelry store in search of a ring, and in the glass case I see a gold ring, which turns out to have an inscription in Greek on one side, and the English translation on the other. There is an older man behind the counter whom I would like to have wait on me, but he is*

133

*busy until later, and I say I will wait. When he does serve
me, I feel embarrassed about buying a wedding ring when I
have no partner, but it seems to be all right.*

The dream ended there, but as I reflected on it, puzzling
over the Greek inscription, I suddenly realized that the
only Greek word I have ever looked up in the dictionary is
TELEIOS, which means "wholeness", or "all-inclusive-
ness", or "completeness". It *doesn't* mean "perfection", as
translated in the New Testament, for the addiction to perfection of which Marion Woodman writes is a trap that
never allows a sense of wholeness. I remember my defini-
tion of maturity at age twenty-one as "being adequate to
every situation" — and what a tyranny that was! I've
learned slowly to be more accepting of the darker side of
me, to be comfortable with "mistakes" and inadequacies,
encouraged by Jung to know that evil is intrinsic to life,
to be transformed in part, but never eliminated. I love one
of his sayings, that "The right way to wholeness is made
up of fateful detours and wrong turnings." There have
been plenty of those in my life.

And so, because the symbol in the dream was so compelling, I had a gold ring made, inscribed with the Greek
letters —t-e-l-e-i-o-s— and with the "translation" as a
symbol: the cross inside a circle. This, too, has meaning as
the acceptance of opposites within the whole. And I wear
it on the wedding ring finger as a commitment to the *inner*
marriage of feminine and masculine qualities — a commitment to the wholeness which is the foundation of any
outer relationship I may enter. And I find that wearing it
is both joyful and helpful.

I think that the Women's Resources Center embodies in
the world this sense of commitment and search for whatever helps women to feel "whole" — hale, healthy, thriv-
ing — and this is my wish for us all in the *next* ten years!

The *inner work* referred to in that anniversary talk was already in
its fourth intensive year. This would prove to be my last major shift
in work in the world. I had found my true vocation, my "calling".
How it came about, the joys and the vicissitudes, belong to the next
chapter.

10

INNER WORK

Tara came into being when the sea of knowledge, of
which she is the quintessence, was churned. ...she
is also the force of the center, which ... presses toward consciousness and knowledge, transformation
and illumination.

Erich Neumann[1]

A person is neither a thing nor a process but an
opening or a clearing through which the Absolute
can manifest.

Martin Heidegger

In the summer of 1978 I turned once again to reading Jungian literature. This time I chose June Singer's *Boundaries of the Soul*.[2] June
Singer is one of the remarkable women writers of my generation, side
by side in my reading experience with Frances Wickes, Esther
Harding, and Marie-Louise von Franz — all of whom have been my
inspiration for decades. This particular book differs from the others
in that it focuses on the analyst's experience of the work of analysis
itself, and now that I had committed myself to the field of therapy, I
read it from that perspective. Half way through the book, I suddenly
realized: *this* is the way I want to be able to work! The awareness

---

[1]Erich Neumann: *The Great Mother.* Bollingen Series XLV11, Princeton
University Press, 1972, p. 333.

[2]June Singer: *Boundaries of the Soul: The Practice of Jung's Psychology*,
(Revised Edition). New York, Anchor Books, 1994.

came as a shock. I was sixty-four. Who was I to presume that I might qualify as an analyst? I would have to ponder the idea, check whether it was a valid desire. This was August.

In September I participated in a workshop with Jean Houston in Santa Cruz, where one of the exercises was to see what the barriers were to our individual creativity. Mine seemed to be the doubting of my own resources...and as I sat quietly asking to let go of this block, an image began to form of a figure, a Presence dimly perceived but very real. When I came home I tried to sketch the figure, a female, seated, Oriental in feeling. I searched Erich Neumann's classic book, *The Great Mother*, and among the large collection of photographs of ancient goddesses I came upon the White Tara. With a sense of recognition I knew that she was the inspiration behind my meditative experience, beckoning me to honor "the force of the center which presses toward consciousness and knowledge, transformation and illumination."[3] Later, I would write this as the frontispiece of my drawing workbook, and search with delight among postcard images for the many interpretations of this figure. She is envisioned as the female counterpart of the Buddha, often painted as the Green Tara. She is one of the pantheon of feminine spiritual beings: Mary, Isis, the Black Madonna, Kuan Yin. My grand-daughter brought me a poster from India of the Green Tara, which is framed and has a place of honor in my living room.

It was in this spirit that I picked up the telephone and told Dr. John Allan I would like to talk with him about training. He was the only Jungian analyst in Vancouver at that time, and I had known him at Family Place. "It just so happens that I have a cancellation tomorrow afternoon at four o'clock. Can you come then?" Indeed I could! John handed me the brochure of the Inter-Regional Society of Jungian Analysts, and we talked about my application. I could begin analysis with him right away. No discussion of cost, or of my age, or of meeting the formal requirements. Just, *Begin*.

The first requisite was one hundred hours of analysis. I had had at least two hundred hours of work thirty years before in Los Angeles, so I wrote Hilda Kirsch and Max Zeller for confirmation. Did they have any record of my hours? Sadly, I learned that both of them had

---

[3]Erich Neumann: *The Great Mother: An Analysis of the Archetype.* Bollingen Series XLV11 Princeton, N.J., Princeton University Press, Paperback Edition 1972, pp. 333-4.

recently died. Lore Zeller, who had been my good friend, wrote that she remembered my working with Max, but there were no records. In the end, The Inter-Regional Society accepted my word, and gave me credit for seventy-five hours, requesting that since the work was so far in the past I do twenty-five with John Allan before applying. This I did. The gods were with me, for today the requirements are more stringent, not only with regard to hours of personal analysis, but to hours of prior supervised practice, professional membership and liability insurance.

"The gods", or "fate", or what David Spangler calls "the formative forces", were supporting my sense of vocation. Spangler describes these forces as

> a flow and process of influence, energy, presence, imagery, and inspiration that manifests something. It gives birth to or shapes an already existing incarnation.[4]

The night before my first analytic session with John Allan I dreamed: *I am wanting to do something for which I need permission, and a figure with a top like a delicately veined fan bows toward me.* Only recently have I connected this figure with the tiny silver pendant which I had bought in Peru, drawn to it by some sense of meaning. I wore this pendant to my admissions interview, feeling it as a talisman in that critical moment. The first question put to me by the analyst on my right, Tom Kapacinskas, was: "What is that pendant you are wearing?" My response: "I don't know. I only know I like it." "Aren't you afraid to wear an image you don't know the meaning of?" "No, I trust its meaning, because it feels right." Later, I consulted Louise Mahdi about its identity, and she could only guess that it was an Incan version of the *anthropos*, the primordial first man. Somehow, without at all understanding the esoteric implications of this figure, I still have a feeling of its androgyny and of its essential sacredness, and I still wear it with pleasure. It was this figure, I think, who came to me in that first dream, as a blessing for my undertaking.

Almost immediately the work centered around the damaged feminine self, and the need for nourishment. I dreamt of a young handicapped woman learning to walk; and of hungry birds circling in

---

[4]David Spangler and William I. Thompson: *Reimagination of the World.* op.cit. p.120.

menacing fashion as I bicycled toward a lodge in the woods, too late for tea. I dreamed of my mother being ill and weak, and of my looking after her. In my first marriage, and in my mothering, I had replicated the depression which I think was always present in my mother; but there had never been consciousness of the connection with her. The first sense of having something positive in common with my mother came with dreams of embroideries — beautiful ethnic, colorful sashes and borders of garments, a handmade jerkin, enameled ceramic buttons, a patterned carpet — which evoked memories of my home. One long richly embroidered sash I wound around me in fantasy, from head to foot, and painted it. One strip had, in the dream, been cut into at one end, and when I discovered I had drawn it with one edge cut off, I found I was not dismayed. "This is the way the design evolved, without intent, with absorption and pleasure. I have no need to mend it. Life is evolving as it should...including whatever damage there has been." So I wrote in my journal.

This was a beginning of recovering a sense of my mother, but I had a great deal of work to do before I could connect with her at a feeling level — the level at which there had been so much damage. Since my tie to her was unconscious, I had first to free myself from the controlling, driving aspect of myself that cut off feeling. A dream in which I was forbidden to enter my mother's bedroom confirmed my inability to make intimate connection. But in the meantime I was able to experience something of the Great Mother, and drew myself as a small person in her arms, pleading, in tears, "Great Mother, hold me!" Sometimes this archetypal level is imaged as a whale, and in a guided fantasy during a lecture I experienced riding in the mouth of a Great Whale with such pleasure and reality that when I "came back" and opened my eyes I was still in the undulation of the sea. Sometimes she is experienced as an old wise woman, as in this dream:

> A man has been searching for a gift for his elderly mother, and shows me a black silk kimono. I say, "It's elegant, but too heavy..." And then later I see her, a tiny, very old Chinese woman wearing a royal blue silk kimono piped in white. She is vividly beautiful, and I am moved by the vision of her.

I painted her — as John Allan always encouraged me to do — and in an analytic session encountered her non-verbally, each of us in a kneeling position, facing each other. There was a sense of peace and serenity and sharing, woman with woman. I felt she had come to help me be in touch with the feminine....There were many such experiences in analysis. I share these to give a sense of the aliveness of the work that I was privileged to do.

The formal aspects of the training were another matter. I will always remember the morning of my admissions interview. April, pouring rain in a lodge in California. At breakfast, seated between June Singer and Werner Engel, a venerable New York analyst , I am captivated by his interest in my experience of Family Place...so captivated that I lose track of time and suddenly discover that it is nine o'clock, the time of my interview! I flee, have trouble finding the room in another building, and walk in to find six men seated around a table, with a large armchair left for me at one end. [Interviewing committees now consist of only three analysts, always including both men and women.] Fortunately, one of the analysts is John Talley from Santa Fe, and we have a friendship with Peggy Church in common. That breaks the ice. Halfway through, James Hall comments: "I had the impression from your letter of intent that you are a feeling type. You don't seem so now." "No", I reply, "when I'm under stress I retreat into my head." Thank goodness I could be honest! Later, someone asks if I had had a dream that night. I had, and I had recorded it, expecting to be asked, but I couldn't remember a thing! Later, upstairs, a wise woman analyst remarked. "The psyche knows what it's doing. You weren't meant to recount that dream to those men!"

The experience of my examination on archetypal material was profound. My journal of April 4, 1981 records:

> Facing the archetypal material is a fearsome unknown. I fell into an abyss late yesterday, back into the old feeling that "I'll never know enough" and ignoring my *experiences* of the archetypes in contrast to book learning. What the "authorities" say is always what's important to know! I ignore the deep inner sense of authority which is now so strong for me...Well, I'm *not* going to do that this morning!

So I got up at five o'clock and listed the many ways in which I had encountered that deeper dimension of life...in the myth of the Wounded Healer and of the Navajo Changing Woman; in the Four Springs seminar with Sheila Moon on The Fool; in dreams of the

139

pearl, the gift of the serpent, the Chinese mother, the Wise Old
Medicine Man stirring the fire in the brazier, the turquoise stone,
the ring and the inner marriage; in the binding commitment urged
by both Jesus and Jung to the Self, the will of God; the sense of kinship with goddess Athena, the "father's daughter".... In the examination room I felt empowered to share this understanding, and felt
heard. John Talley asked about a fairy tale, and I mentioned one that
I felt connected with, "The Two Ferdinands". John wasn't familiar
with it; "Can you tell us the tale?" To my amazement, I, who never
was a story-teller, told the tale with gusto, remembering all the details except the last one, and enjoying the whole experience. That
exam got top marks, in contrast to the clinical one where I got caught
in lack of specific knowledge of the DSM3 (the 1980 Manual of the
American Psychiatric Association) and barely passed. Clearly, in that
area experience must be complemented by knowledge.

After the exams, John Allan indicated he would discontinue analytic work, and I searched for a way to continue analysis and training. I reached out to analysts in San Francisco, and in Santa Fe, but
in the end knew that the more complex transportation made those
plans unfeasible. Fortunately, Toronto was a possible destination.
Marion Woodman was willing to work with me in analysis, and
Fraser Boa in supervision. So for eight months I flew to Toronto once
a month, saw Marion for five hours and Fraser for four, and flew
home again. At my last session with Fraser, I collapsed into his huge
armchair, exhausted. Fraser took one look at me, and said: "Why are
you doing this to yourself? The certificate isn't worth the paper it's
printed on!" Startled, I knew that this arduous way of being trained
was not what my psyche wanted for me. It was reinforcing the old
driven, ambitious side that ignored the feminine. So I took a leave of
absence for six months, and returned only when I knew that writing
the case studies would be valuable, and that I could do them at my
own speed, separating that exam from the writing and defence of the
thesis.

Nevertheless, those eight months with Marion Woodman were
priceless, as anyone who knows her will understand. Her books, *Addiction to Perfection, The Pregnant Virgin* and *The Ravaged Bridegroom*[5] all write of the problem that was mine: of redeeming the deep
feminine, the principle of relatedness to the soul. This only comes

---

[5]All published by Inner City Books, Toronto.

about with freeing the psyche from the thraldom of a controlling masculine principle — a pseudo-masculinity that damages men as well as women. We are familiar today with the overt types of abuse inflicted by fathers, but not so familiar with the more subtle, unconscious ties with absent or idealized fathers, or those whose inadequate relationships with their wives lead them to project their sexual feeling, unconsciously, onto a loved daughter. Bound by that kind of tie, the daughter may spend a lifetime trying fruitlessly first to please her father, and then searching equally fruitlessly, equally unconsciously, to find a partner who matches the projection of the ideal man. Marion helped me first to be aware of this, and then, through dreams, to experience the tie and break it. Even with all that work, it requires a constant effort to be conscious of the pattern in order not to continue the projection. I'm not always successful. Only as I continue moving toward inner feminine authority does the old pattern fade.

Many analysts have written about learning from their clients, and I have too. On one occasion, having experienced negative transference [the anger transferred from a client's internalized parent to the analyst] I was able to express for the first time, in active imagination[6], my anger at my own mother. I record that piece of work because it embodies so many of the issues women experience.

> It's not *fair* to be angry with me! It's because you're angry with Daddy, and you take it out on me...and I'm angry with you for being always tired and depressed and anxious...It's not *fair* that I can't make a noise, or be angry, or have lots of friends at the house, or make a mess — just because you're such a fuss and a perfectionist and have a bad heart. I don't *want* you to be like that! I want you to be *well* and to play with me, and to laugh, and to be affectionate with Daddy, and to hug me. You're always saying: "Watch out! Be careful! Don't do that! You're bothering me!"

> Dear Great Mother, I want your generous arms, and your continuing Presence, and your heartiness, and your lust for Life! I want *all* of you, inside me — the ability to

[6]See Glossary. For further study see Robert A. Johnson: *Inner Work: Using Dreams and Active Imagination for Personal Growth.* San Francisco, Harper & Row, 1986.

love *and* to be angry — in every cell of my body...You *are* here, more and more, as I learn to play, and feel undefensive, and glad to be me. And I give you thanks for "mirroring" me now...that I so often feel "the gleam in your eye".

Two dreams seemed to conclude the work in reclaiming Mother. One was of finding one of my mother's silver knives, and *her* mother's silver butter dish — after which I got her flatware out of storage and began to use it with pleasure. The other was of finding, in the hollow of the Sacred Mountain, a clay figure of mother and child which has survived destruction "at the hands of the white man" and is identified by a silver plaque. I modeled the figure lovingly, and it has a place on my altar.

It was while I was reviewing my six years of work in the training program that I realized that the work with active imagination, painting and clay modeling, had been invaluable in helping me to let go of my over-riding thinking function and to get in touch with my natural feeling. This is the most powerful tool I know for taking seriously the clues from the realm of what has been beyond consciousness, to claiming rejected and unknown parts of ourselves as *ours*. The power of the image manifested there in paint or clay is doubled or redoubled in potency, and speaks to the ego more irresistibly. For me, the painting of a key in the lock of a sports car convertible opened the domain of pleasure in a work-addicted life. The dream of a little girl lighting a tiny fir tree, dancing around it at midnight with her imaginary playmates, and giving the dreamer a candle to commemorate the event, led to a painting and a ritual of lighting the Tree of Life. The figure of the unknown man who was "the ultimate in contained pain", staring starkly from a white page, *demanded* that attention be paid to the drivenness so characteristic of the professional woman who is a father's daughter.

As images come alive, and in their wake the feeling function intensifies, the confusions around "masculine" and "feminine" ask to be clarified. These are not gender-related attributes. In a seminar at U.B.C. on *The Way of the Dream*[7] Dr. John Allan pointed out that these are simply two different kinds of energies. Just as I associated

---

[7]*The Way of the Dream*: Dr. Marie-Louise von Franz in conversation with Fraser Boa. Toronto, ON, Windrose Films Ltd., 1988.

Sun to father and Moon to mother, their earliest coloration is supplied by the parents, and by the ways in which the parents manifest their energies. My father held center stage, while my mother was unable to provide a model of feminine fulfillment. My guess is that wherever the father is idealized the mother will be negated in some fashion: the Sun will eclipse the Moon and the daughter will have the life task of bringing these values into balance.

When I graduated from training April 27, 1985, Frank and Sheila gave me a moonstone pendant and earrings, and a beautiful card by a Kwa-Gulth artist, Stanley Hunt, titled "Moon". Sheila wrote a poem:

> For us,
> this pendant
> is a symbol
> of your journey
> to reclaim your feminine Self.
>
> Your path
> has been long and winding,
> your search
> growing broader with the years,
> and yet
> your direction clear.
>
> Your moon,
> once eclipsed by the sun,
> now stands
> in new relation to it —
> connected,
> yet
> distinct.
>
> Your moon,
> once hidden,
> now stands
> for all to see —
> radiant
> in its beauty
> and wholeness.

What a gift...What an affirmation!

Another miraculous aspect of working with dreams in analysis is the appearance of symbols of the Self at moments of intense struggle. We are all familiar with Jesus' symbols of the pearl of great price, and the treasure hidden in the field. The numinosity of these symbols as they appear may linger for days, or for years: *A serpent drops a pearl into my hands; flowers grow on a barren tree; heavenly music sounds; a golden child appears.* Marie-Louise von Franz, writing about the withdrawl of projections, says:

> The possibility of integrating projected contents...does not arise until symbols of the Self begin to appear. From this center impulses proceed to a contemplative, thoughtful re-collection of the personality."[8]

I wrote about the "inner marriage" in the story of the dream of the ring, shared at the Women's Resources Center anniversary. This is related to the reclaimed feminine, working in tandem with a new-found masculine that can function with a sense both of initiative and of relatedness. I have a sense of mystery and of gratitude that my life granted me the possibility of taking this path. The ego has a role to play in responding to the proffered choices; but the *grace* to choose wisely, and the *opportunity* for choice, are the gift of God. Jung describes this mystery as the "transcendent function".[9]

> Once the unconscious content has been given form and the meaning of the formulation is understood, the question arises as to how the ego will relate to this position, and how the ego and the unconscious are to come to terms. This is the second and more important stage of the procedure, the bringing together of opposites for the production of a third: the transcendent function. At this stage it is no longer the unconscious that takes the lead, but the ego...[10]

For me, the ability of the ego to take the lead was made possible, I think, by the many seminars on The Records of the Life of Jesus, and the reality of the commitment to "do the will of God". Even in the

---

[8]Marie-Louise von Franz: *Projection and Re-Collection in Jungian Psychology: Reflections of the Soul*. La Salle, Open Court Publishing Company, 1980.
[9]See Glossary.
[10]Carl Jung: *Collected Works*, v.8, par.181.

darkest moments it never occurred to me to doubt the direction of that commitment: to seek to know the better alternative and to act on it. It is clear that I didn't always perceive the wise alternative; blindness blocked the perception of the better way. Indeed, it is not given to the ego always to know what choice would lead directly to a fuller life; often it has to detour through painful experience in order to gain in depth and consciousness. But it is the *commitment* that enables the "fateful detours and wrong turnings" to become compost for wholeness. This is the path of individuation.[11]

The Jungian training occupied the years from 1979 to 1985. When it came time to write my thesis, I was turning seventy. I don't think I ever planned a birthday party with a greater sense of celebration. Those "goodly threescore years and ten" had been so greatly enriched by the challenges and inspiration of the training that for my thesis I wanted to explore my own autobiography as a study of psyche's journey toward oneSelf — a proposal very reluctantly accepted by my committee of analysts. "Not appropriate for a thesis...not a contribution to Jungian thought", they objected. Stubbornly, I persuaded them that the exploration in depth of one woman's journals and dreams could be educational if the transformation of life patterns could be documented in a grounded way. I was able to do this. The project might have foundered without the twelve pages of radical criticism and suggestions for change offered by analyst William Walker of Memphis, Tennessee. With the aid of a computer consultant I turned chapters upside down, but stuck to my sense of the personal journal as essential. Dreams highlighted the themes of a long life. Mythology revealed my mother in the goddess Hestia. Astrology — Liz Greene's book on Saturn[12] — illumined my "leaden", serious nature. The literature on fathers' daughters showed me I was not alone in my search for my own feminine path. In the end, I felt it had been for me "the icing on the cake", the one thing needful to complement my analytic work.

I even managed an academic justification for using "an n of 1" — that is, a study of a single subject. At the very end of the writing I came "by chance" upon a book by two social scientists[13] who de-

---

[11]See Glossary.

[12]Liz Greene: *Saturn: a new look at an old devil.* Samuel Weiser, Inc., New York, 1976.

[13]Ian I. Mitroff and Ralph H. Kilmann: *Methodological Approaches to Social Science.* San Francisco, Jossey-Bass, 1978.

scribe quite precisely what I experienced as my approach to my thesis, and who — incredible as it may seem — came to their classification of the range of approaches adopted by scientists through their examination of Jung's typology and the "logic" of mythical thought. Their work focuses on the challenge of incorporating the feeling function into scientific research. I was astonished and encouraged to find myself mirrored in the Table 4 descriptors, including: "Preferred mode of inquiry: the case study; the in-depth study of a particular individual." The exhilaration I had experienced in the writing reminded me of the intellectual satisfaction of my doctoral thesis — perhaps all the more exciting when one is *not* primarily a thinking type and has reclaimed her feeling side.

Recently, as I was placing accumulated snapshots in an album, I came across pictures from those years and remembered that in the midst of the intense training were other pleasures and adventures. A group of a dozen or so good friends celebrated each other's birthdays with gatherings in our homes — good food, laughter and affection are evident in the pictures. Five of the women met for dinner each month, at one time in a Greek restaurant where the calamari was delicious, and we still meet (now only four) and call ourselves the Calamari, sharing a remarkable closeness over many years. They are all much younger than I, and help to keep me young in spirit and to feel cared for as energies fail. I am indeed blessed in my friends.

The adventures belong to travel. Every year I went to Jungian conferences in Quebec, Pittsburgh, Chicago, San Francisco, Santa Fe, the Bahamas. Three times training took me to Switzerland, either to Kusnacht where the Jung Institute is located, or to Zurich. The wonderful network of trains allowed me to explore small towns such as Einsiedeln where there is a shrine of the Black Virgin, or Sils Maria in the southern Alps, and the larger cities of Berne and Basel. Following one winter seminar I took the train to Vienna and landed in such a snowstorm that I spent my three days trudging in deep snow, and on Sunday morning made my way to a baroque cathedral so cold inside that I couldn't stay through the service! I did manage to get to a concert and to see the famous dancing horses.

One series of snapshots is labelled a "mini Sabbatical" and follows my solitary travel by train across parts of Germany and France and the Colmar region of vineyards and the stork sanctuary. En route to Paris I lost my wallet, and spent much of my time in that city haunting the Eurorail office until they replaced my pass. But in Notre

Dame I lit a candle for Auntie Grace, whose generosity had financed the trip. I also came upon a smaller cathedral close by where the serenity of the atmosphere prompted me to try to express to the pale-faced priest how moved I was by this calm in contrast to the busyness of Notre Dame. There, too, I took a picture of a very old wooden statue of a young virgin with a basket of wheat sheaves, an ancient depiction of the goddess.

Travelling as a wanderer, without reservations, was sometimes lonely, and I remember the discomfort of being a single woman, sitting alone in a formal dining room in Chartres, the object of scrutiny from couples at nearby tables. Going out at night also felt problematical, and I spent many evenings buried in Peter Matthiessen's book, *The Snow Leopard*[14], and writing in my journal. Daytime joys compensated. At four o'clock one afternoon I walked to Chartres Cathedral and found it blessedly empty except for a young woman seated on the altar steps, playing her violin. Entranced, I listened for a long time to the rapturous sound as it circled the high-vaulted ceiling. I think she must have felt akin to Paul Horn's joy when he played his flute in the Taj Mahal. The spring after graduation, 1986, I joined a Citizen Diplomat tour to the Soviet Union organized by the Institute of Noetic Sciences. Friends were surprised at my enthusiasm: "You've never talked about Russia before!" I hadn't known myself what a deep sense of connection would emerge as I travelled there and felt myself responding to the very soul of that nation in its yearning for their ideal communism. When I went to Peru I had no conscious purpose other than a holiday with friends; and travels to Europe had been mostly to experience travel for its own sake. But this trip was organized as an opportunity to extend friendship to people of a struggling nation, and was led by a young woman, Sharon Tennison, who had made ten previous trips and come to know, and to be trusted by, many individual groups, including the official agency Intourist. So in addition to experiencing the visual wonders of Russia, we met in a number of homes for private discussion, and with several Friendship groups very concerned about peace. I remember one poignant evening returning to the hotel from an adult education meeting where we had talked freely about world events. A young man walked with me all the way, speaking earnestly in a low voice of his unhappiness. There was no counselling avail-

---

[14]Peter Matthiessen: *The Snow Leopard*. New York, Viking, 1978.

able, and he finally asked: "Do you think it's wrong to be depressed?" I assured him it was not, and when we parted we embraced.

The everyday scenes were drab in midwinter, people bundled in dark clothes with little color. But in Sochi, the health resort on the Black Sea where people were on holiday, the mood was lively. In the cafeteria of the sanitarium which we visited, many were ready to dance, to make music, to try to make conversation in spite of the language barrier. In a Ukrainian restaurant in Kiev middle-aged couples were dancing to fast-paced, exuberant music, the men often more expressive than the women when it came to kissing on the dance floor! I realized that for Soviets the public street is not the place to be expressive.

I was very moved by the scenes in the churches which were always crowded with worshipers, and rich with color and music. The visual beauty, the reds and golds of the icons, was breathtaking. We travelled to the only surviving seminary at Zagorsk where even in mid-week and freezing cold Russians were worshiping. In one of the churches there, people were lined up to go one by one before the shrine of St. Sergius, a 14th century monk, to kneel and pray while a priest at the foot of the tomb chanted quietly.... Some of us attended the Sunday service at the Baptist church in Moscow where every seat was taken, people were standing four-deep in the center aisle and two-deep in the side aisles right to the doors — standing through the two-hour service! Over an hour of that time was filled with glorious music. As far as we could learn from discussions, there was no longer any problem about attending church, although active membership would probably preclude advancing to management or leadership in the Party.

What impressed me, in addition to the unforgettable visual images of art and architecture, was the availability of free post-secondary education, and of free day care. We talked with an American woman who had married a Soviet, been divorced, returned to the United States...and then returned to Russia, because, as she told us, she realized that as a single mother she would be "better off where there would be no pornography, the streets would be safe for my children, there would be good day care, and I could return to University to complete my degree without constant worry about supporting the children, or health care, or unemployment." She had been back eleven years, and was "content".

My "Notes from Russia" report that en route home

> I am still reeling from the impact of Russia on me. It is as if part of me has identified with their struggle...as if "we have seen the enemy, and the enemy is US." The enemy for all of us is poverty and ignorance and greed and corruption — and they are struggling in their own way to solve the residue of centuries of exploitation of one large group by another small group. And we are struggling for a better life in another way.

I am sad as I read these notes. The "experiment" failed in so many respects; greed and crime surfaced when the rigid repression was lifted and people were unready for responsibility. We were so hopeful about Gorbachev; and now the disintegration under the influence of global restructuring is disastrous.

Three years after this journey to Russia, in 1989 when the Jungian Congress held its triennial Congress in Paris, I invited my sixteen-year-old grand-daughter Katryn to share this trip with me. We began in Geneva where she wanted to visit the headquarters of the World Council of Churches, went on to Florence, and thence into France, to the Riviera, where she swam in the Mediterranean. We crossed France slowly by train, spending one glorious night in a small castle, and then went all the way out to Cape Breton (more swimming, this time in the Atlantic) where we rented a car. Katryn was a good navigator since she is fully bilingual, and we loved the northern countryside as we sped toward the cathedral, Mont St. Michel. August tourists jammed that ancient site, and we bypassed the tour and joined a small group in the chapel for a moving service. We drove on to the Normandy beaches, and Katryn swam there one afternoon while I rested at the bed-and-breakfast home in the country. One of my most memorable images is of the new cathedral commemorating Joan of Arc, built as an upside-down fisherman's boat with the utmost simplicity. A sign requested silence, for which I was grateful. Much as I loved the great cathedrals there were usually too many people for me to enjoy their spaciousness.

In Paris we shared some of the Congress lectures, and then Katryn took off on her own to explore the city. One evening we were guests, along with other participants, in the home of an analyst living outside the city...an evening I shall never forget. We were divided into two tables — those who spoke mostly English and those who knew only French with a smattering of English. Katryn joined that table, and I learned later that she had been the translator, charming everyone with her ease in helping people understand each other. The other memorable aspect of that evening was the food: the variety, the endless courses, the wines, and to cap it all off, an enormous mound of exotic fruits.... Altogether, an unforgettable four weeks.

* * * * *

From the time I entered training until retirement in 1993 I was always involved with Jungian educational activities in the wider world. Locally, a group of friends interested in Jung organized the C.G. Jung Society of Vancouver, which continues to sponsor occasional lectures. While Anne Ironside was director of programming for the Center for Continuing Education at U.B.C. we had her full support for presenting lectures and workshops in that setting, and they were always fully booked. We are not so fortunate now. Concerned that serious students should have some background in the *Collected Works* should they wish to train as analysts, I began a Jung Intensive Study Group in my home. One of the criteria for membership was to be in analysis so that the study would not be purely intellectual, and that group continued into a fifth year. Many friendships were formed, and one member, Sharon Driscoll, is now (1996) entering her fourth year of analytic training with Jungian Analysts • North Pacific. Another is planning to train. Cam Trowsdale, by profession a violinist, has done an exhaustive study of Jungian typology which deserves to be a book. From a second such study group three members are now studying at the Jung Institute in Zurich; one, a physician, is completing his doctorate in depth psychology at Pacifica Institute; and another physician is incorporating Jungian insights into his regular medical practice. Sheila Fodchuk has spearheaded the development of the Cathedral Center for Spiritual Direction and is its senior Director. Every member is following a creative path. I have been stimulated and nourished by all these remarkable people.

The continental organization with which I trained, the Inter-Regional Society of Jungian Analysts, was growing in influence and maturity and I happily participated in their development. While

Terrill Gibson and I were still candidates we set up a special room at the national conference where applicants and trainees could gather between interviews and examinations for supportive conversation and snacks. These periods were so stressful that this was much appreciated and became established as a regular practice. Through those gatherings I came to know many remarkable candidates who have gone on to write and teach. I never ran for office, but did volunteer as an examiner one year, and served as advisor for Dr. Margret Bridgford's thesis — both enriching experiences. As our regional organization, the Pacific Northwest Society, gradually became more active, I reported on their activities at each conference, and was eagerly looking forward to establishing a training program.

Unfortunately, as often happens in organizations with intensely focused concerns, there were sharp disagreements in philosophy and personal antagonisms. At one crucial meeting of the Society in April 1991, after yet another split vote and unacceptable regulations affecting new members, seven of us resigned in a body, prepared to form a new organization closer to what we perceived to be commitment to the individual psyche and more flexible in the design of training. Sadly, this led to bitter feelings and an effort to block our right to establish a second society within the region. Ladson Hinton and I, as President and Vice-President, travelled twice to Chicago to defend our position before the National Association of Jungian Societies, and were successful — partly, I think, because we remained quietly non-defensive and non-hostile.

We did, in fact, create a very different kind of analyst organization, and with great care have maintained a structure that is democratic and warm in tone. A year later, at the International Congress in Chicago, we were admitted as an official society, Jungian Analysts • North Pacific, and celebrated! Immediately, we turned our attention to designing a training program, each of us making thoughtful input, discussing thoroughly each step, and then critiquing the final written version. We have called it "A Program of Analyst Education", and the position of "Director of Training" is re-named the Director of Education — terminology that expresses our philosophy. In the final two years the general program of monthly or bi-monthly seminars and colloquia becomes truly an individual program, allowing each candidate to proceed in terms of talents, interests, and deficits, designing the final phase with the guidance of the Education Committee. We have learned from many other societies, especially in the creation of the Guidelines for the Ethics and Well-Being Committee. We are concerned that people be "heard", not only in individual cases, but in registered complaints where we firmly believe that mediation rather than litigation is the preferred mode.

These years have been exciting, challenging, and exhausting. I participated in the interviewing and admission of our first seven candidates, and still serve as Secretary of Jungian Analysts • North Pacific, and now also as Vice-President of the North Pacific Institute for Analytical Psychology, the educational arm of the Society. It has been infinitely rewarding to be part of these new ventures, and to continue to participate in their evolution. One of the happiest aspects is my deepening friendship with Ladson and Darlene Hinton, who have opened their hearts and their home to me whenever I go to Seattle for meetings. Darlene prepares my room with flowers from her garden and pampers me with gourmet food. Ladson is psychoanalyst, psychiatrist and Jungian analyst, with the wisdom born of long years of clinical experience, wide reading, and reflection. I learn continually from Ladson. He and I have worked so closely together for the last five years that I feel he knows me better than any other colleague, and his high regard means a great deal.

Although I retired officially in 1993, I resumed a very small analytic practice a year later, coaxed by someone who was determined to work with a woman analyst, and at present I am the only one in Vancouver. Late in 1995 I accepted two more analysands. Enough! Driving to Seattle has become too tiring, and I take the bus. An aging body and limited vision are taking their toll.

The aging process is one of the Dragons to be met on the Journey, and my efforts to come to terms with this Character occupy the remaining chapters.

11

Body and Soul

Choose life—only that and always, and at whatever risk.
To let life leak out, to let it wear away by the mere passage of time, to withhold giving it and spreading it is to
choose nothing.

Sister Helen Kelley

May Sarton's journal, *At Seventy*[1], chronicles the year in which
she turned seventy — 1982. The jacket description reports:

> Here she relishes what she feels at seventy: not old, still
> looking forward with joy, acknowledging the realization
> that all the good and the bad, the joy and the pain of life
> have 'woven a rich tapestry and given food to grow on'
> into the future. 'Why is it good to be old?' she was asked
> at one of her lectures. 'Because,' she said, ' I am more my-
> self than I have ever been.'

I echo her experience, line by line. The years from graduation
from training until I turned eighty were not only productive and
satisfying, but a time when I earned a good living for the first time in
my life! And I spent much of what I earned on sheer enjoyment:
books, concerts, travel and my home. I appreciated being able to be
more generous with gifts, not only for friends but for some twenty
organizations doing in the world what I, physically, was unable to
do. My analytic practice was full; I had a waiting list.

---

[1]May Sarton: *At Seventy*. New York, Norton and Company, 1984.

At seventy-seven I finally became aware of slowing energies and decided not to accept new clients, but to continue with the ones I had until they completed their work or until I had to stop work. I always thought that I would work on at least until ninety like those women around Jung — Esther Harding, Frances Wickes, Barbara Hannah. These were my mentors. In some ways the very idea was a taskmaster, and my body began to register a complaint. My back, strained from a lifelong curvature, seemed not to want to hold me up, and my legs objected to stairs. A neurologist concluded it was "the aging process" and I would have to live with it. Not willing to settle for such a verdict, I worked in therapeutic yoga and with alternative healers, with some success, at least temporarily.

On my seventy-ninth birthday my very dear friend, Sylvia Ommanney, said she wanted to nominate me for one of the "Women of Distinction" awards from the Vancouver YWCA. I was startled, and touched that she would think of such a thing — and go to the enormous trouble of collecting letters of endorsement. Of the eight categories that covered areas such as art, business, sports, commu-

Sylvia Ommanney and Clare at
"Women of Distinction" Award Dinner, May 27, 1993

nity service, mine was "Education, Training and Development". Sylvia collected a dozen letters, duplicated them, and bound them in a volume which she covered in dark blue raw silk, embroidered with my initials. Friends and colleagues, all the way back to university days, had written about projects which I had undertaken which seemed to fill a need in the community. I was deeply moved. Until

John Milsum, Judith Nelson, Sheila McFadzean, Anne Ironside, Clare, Suyin Lee, Sylvia Ommanney and Frank Harris

Anne Ironside, John Milsum and Suyin Lee

155

then I think I had not realized this had been a lifelong theme, a series of pursuits which had yielded such enormous satisfaction.

We didn't know, until the night of the banquet, May 27, 1993, whether I would be selected from the group of nominees in my category. Sylvia had arranged a table of friends (who paid dearly for the privilege, I might add) that included my son Frank and his wife, Sheila, Anne Ironside, Suyin Lee, John Milsum, Judith Nelson and herself. One by one the winners were named, and their photographs projected on the large screens at each side of the banquet hall where a thousand guests cheered the lucky ones. We were tense with excitement. Finally the host began reading the profile we recognized as mine, and we were overcome with jubilation. I had to make my way from a far side, facing into floodlights, up the steps to the podium, and make a speech of acceptance. I think sheer joy overcame nervousness. The occasion coincided with seeing my last client, and entering retirement — and what an appreciative conclusion to a long life in the world!

The last two years of intensive involvement in the development of the Jungian training program had demanded more of my body than I realized, and I was indeed exhausted, although not feeling "burnt out". I gave myself the gift of a cruise to Alaska on a luxury liner — something foreign to me and that I would not want to repeat even if I could afford it. But the scenery was magnificent, and I spent hours on deck just relishing the beauty of mountains, glaciers, and the sea.

Those last two years of strenuous work were, I suspect, borrowed from what would have been a move into greater focus on the interior realm of spiritual development. And in the fall I approached this long-felt need as yet another project. To move into the realm of the spiritual can mean many things. Many biographies and autobiographies, especially Lama Govinda's *The Way of the White Clouds*[2], had been both inspiration and challenge. The title of this last book is itself evocative. In the Foreword Peter Matthiessen explains that

> White clouds drift everywhere through Buddhist symbology, wandering through the sky leaving no trace. And the sky itself, like the empty mirror, is a symbol of *sunyata*, that so-called "emptiness" or ultimate reality, the eternal essence of the universe. (Page xi)

[2]Lama Anagarika Govinda: *The Way of the White Clouds: A Buddhist Pilgrim in Tibet*. Boston, Shambala, 1988.

This was my first introduction to Buddhist thought, and I responded with deep satisfaction to the story of a very long personal journey, written as autobiography. It was vivid with illustrations of relationships to landscape and the Wise Ones he and his wife met as they travelled. His closing Invocation "To the Buddha of Infinite Light" is for me a prayer. I quote the first stanza:

> Thou who liveth within my heart,
> Awaken me to the immensity of thy spirit,
> To the experience of thy living presence!
> Deliver me from the bonds of desire,
> From the slavery of small aims,
> From the delusion of narrow egohood! (Page 287)

The only clear notion I had at this time was of the need to develop a disciplined practice of meditation, and so I began exploring books on *vipassana* meditation and read with special delight Jack Kornfield's last writing on *A Path With Heart*.[3] This I followed with *Gathering the Light: A Psychology of Meditation* by Jungian analyst V. Walter Odajnyk[4], which helped me to integrate my orientation to Jung with more Western approaches to Buddhism. And then came Sogyal Rinpoche's bestseller, *The Tibetan Book of Living and Dying*.[5] The idea that one needs to *prepare* for dying startled me. I've always looked forward to what I somehow knew from adolescence was a transition to a larger life. But I had never taken seriously the Tibetan concept of the *Bardos* , which I had encountered some time before in Jung's Introduction to *The Tibetan Book of the Dead*. The *Bardos* describe the state of being immediately following death, the confusing nature of the transition from this life to the next, and the danger of getting "lost" in those realms if death comes when the mind is not ready.

The Rinpoche's book had been given me by a good friend, Diane Marshall, who, with Suyin Lee, had met Sogyal Rinpoche in Montreal in the summer and been deeply impressed. So the three of us journeyed to the Mount Madonna center in California for a nine-

---

[3]Jack Kornfield: *A Path With Heart: A Guide Through the Perils and Promises of Spiritual Life*. New York, Bantam Books, 1993.

[4]V. Walter Odajnyk: *Gathering the Light: A Psychology of Meditation*. Boston, Shambala, 1993.

[5]Sogyal Rinpoche: *The Tibetan Book of Living and Dying*. Harper, 1992.

day retreat based on his book and led by the Rinpoche himself. Over five hundred people met in a cold gym where we sat on the floor for hours at a time, my back complaining mightily. Fascinating and inspiring as it was, the Tibetan approach was too culturally based for me. In the long meditation sittings I found myself recognizing that despite Christian theology I do indeed belong to that tradition, and that Jesus is the Buddha of my choice. Perhaps I should have known this, having studied Jesus as teacher in those many seminars on the Records. But it had not seemed possible to find a community of people who honor him in that light, free of dogmatism, and from the perspective of a universal religious longing to *experience* the sense of the Divine within one's own being — what Jesus called living "abundantly". I had stopped attending the Unitarian Church because little attention was paid to Jesus, and intellect seemed so much more important than soul and spirit. I longed for a place where worship was predominant.

Back at home I continued my efforts to meditate in true Buddhist fashion, letting thoughts pass by. One morning I found my thoughts wandering to the questionnaire from the Unitarian Church asking members what they would like to volunteer for. And to my surprise, there I was checking off all the items that had to do with worship: to help plan services, to do readings, to work on the Worship Committee. I even found myself in the pulpit delivering a sermon and remembering with pleasure the year (1965-6) I had worked as Phillip Hewett's assistant and conducted many services. A few days later I recalled that at age twenty I had, for a brief time, decided to enter the ministry. Was *this* to be my focus in retirement?

I did join the Worship Committee. I read a selection from Thich Nhat Hanh at the Watchnight service that New Year's Eve, and offered to conduct a summer service, the period when the minister is on vacation. I began attending church regularly, and was surprised at the renewed strength of the feeling: This is my church. We had been without a settled minister since Phillip Hewett's retirement; and in the spring of 1994 the congregation rejoiced in calling a woman, Rev. Sydney Morris, to that post. Phillip had told me of the resurgence of a desire for more emphasis on spirituality, and that is indeed happening. A renaissance is under way and I rejoice in being part of it.

In the old style of becoming involved in a project that engaged and challenged, my mind and heart once again led me into new areas, and although I rested more, all my energies became focused on spiritual development in relation to the church. It seems very hard for me to overcome the prevalent split in our culture between mind and body; I rocket back and forth between mental excitement and physical weariness. New learning always beckons. This time, in the direction of quantum physics and its import for spirituality.

The search began with a phrase from a Tibetan prayer: "May I remember my true nature." I found myself stumbling so often over the words *my true nature* that I felt a need to find sources in recent Western science that might help me articulate what our human nature actually is, and what may be our connection with the Mystery called God. I've always had what psychologist Eugene Gendlin calls "a felt sense" of that connection, but I wanted words for it, scientific words. My long awareness of the unconscious as revealed by Jung, who used the rhizome as a metaphor for the Self in its invisible relationship with the earth, and my work with dreams, provided a background of experience of something More...but I was reaching for understanding of the vastness of that More in the cosmos itself as revealed by the "new" science. The Jungian journal, *Psychological Perspectives*[6] which is edited by Ernest Rossi, had introduced me to many of the figures writing in this field — David Bohm, Rupert Sheldrake, Ilya Prigogine. Now I turned to a recent book by Danah Zohar, *The Quantum Self: Human Nature and Consciousness Defined by the New Physics.*[7] She says of these inter-connections:

> Things and events once conceived of as separate, parted in both space and time, are seen by the quantum theorist as so integrally linked that their bond mocks the reality of both space and time. They behave, instead, as multiple aspects of some larger whole, their 'individual' existences deriving both their definition and their meaning from that whole. (p.34)

---

[6] Publilshed semi-annually by the C.G. Jung Institute of Los Angeles, 10349 West Pico Blvd., Los Angeles, CA 90064. The sub-title describes its focus: "*A Journal of Global Consciousness Integrating Psyche, Soul, and Nature.*"

[7] Danah Zohar: *The Quantum Self.* New York, Quill/William Morrow, 1990.

Another aspect of quantum theory which validated my sense of prayer is what is referred to as *non-locality* — the instantaneous action-at-a-distance in the absence of a local cause. Rupert Sheldrake writes:

> The traditional belief in prayer is that praying for people who are in distant places...or any kind of intercessory or petitionary prayer, can actually have an effect, by whatever means, at a distance... [If] prayer functions in a manner that it is believed to function, then it must involve action that takes place at a distance, either an action of the mind via its extension, as I've suggested, or an action of a spiritual agency. It may be that we are connected with everybody we think about and all the places we are attached to through our extended minds. Our minds, in fact, may be vast, far-reaching spatially extended networks of connection in space and time — networks of immense scope in which the brains inside our heads are but a portion.[8]

Another fascinating source of documentation for what is "my true nature" is the very readable book by Malcom Talbot, *The Holographic Universe*.[9] The evidence for our connection to the unseen world piles up from numberless intriguing researches: Out-of-Body experiences, Near-Death experiences, reincarnation, shamanism, the work of Stanislav Grof with intra-uterine memories. And there are extraordinary similarities in these records (especially of dazzling light) that complement what is hypothesized by physicists *and* that parallel the reports of mystics from every age and culture.

More recently I read Fred Alan Wolf's latest book, *The Dreaming Universe*[10], and was intrigued by his understanding of dreaming in relation to these imaginal realm experiences. Not only does he see that "dreaming is a necessary part of consciousness that enables the dreamer to develop a higher self-awareness" — as Jung would agree; but that dreaming creates the first self-nonself split to occur in mat-

---

[8]Rupert Sheldrake, "Extended Mind, Power & Prayer", *Psychological Perspectives* 19, 1, 1986.

[9]Michael Talbot: *The Holographic Universe*. HarperPerennial, 1991.

[10]Fred Alan Wolf: *The Dreaming Universe*. New York, Simon & Shuster, 1994.

ter, the differentiation of self and object. "Thus, the material universe dreams to become aware of itself." (p. 20-21) Again,

> The dream is the experimental landscape of the movement of the mind, just as 'out there' waking reality is the experimental landscape of the movement of the body. (p.319)

These were new ideas to me, and exciting. Yet the concept of The Great Dreamer is also a very ancient idea, especially among the aboriginals of Australia whose creation-evolution story is about this Dreamer who dreams the universe into existence. Wolf also quotes (p.175) Thomas Mann, from *The Magic Mountain:*

> Now I know that it is not out of our single souls that we dream. We dream anonymously and communally, if each after his own fashion. The great soul of which we are a part may dream through us, in our manner of dreaming, its own secret dreams, of its youth, its hope, its joy and peace — and its blood sacrifice.[11]

I feel so grateful to the Dreamer who led me to do this reading! It has provided a pathway to living in a larger universe, to a richer inner life. There have been so many opportunities knocking at my door...and yet another one came with a Jung Society lecture and seminar by another quantum physicist, John Hitchcock, and the introduction to his book, *The Web of the Universe: Jung, The "New Physics", and Human Spirituality.*[12] Dr. Hitchcock and John Petroni were doing a ten-day seminar at Four Springs later in the fall entitled "Lead into Gold: the Transformation Process" — and I went, knowing that this would challenge me to greater spiritual depth. I was not disappointed.

The symbolism of the seminar was from alchemy, the medieval search for the Philosopher's Stone — an image parallel to Jesus' image of "the Pearl of Great Price" — disguised by the old alchemists as an effort to transmute lead into gold. Jung's mature writing in his eighties was inspired by this ancient body of knowledge, and com-

---

[11]Fred Alan Wolf: *The Dreaming Universe.* New York, Simon & Shuster, 1994.

[12]John Hitchcock: *The Web of the Universe: Jung, "The New Physics", and Human Spirituality.* New York, Paulist Press, 1991.

plex and mystical as it is, the process of psychological transformation derived from this study is profound. We meditated on, wrote about, and discussed many symbols — lead, silver, fire, the Dragon. One assignment was to write a letter from the Dragon to oneself, and that fiery old character gave me a dressing down. My journal records, in part:

> You haven't paid attention to me ! I could have made you *see* what was going on with those parents. If you'd listened to me you would have asked questions — it's *dumb* not to ask questions ! You just sat on your feelings and looked sweet and worked hard at being a good girl. You nearly smothered me, and I smouldered and squirmed inside you. It's a wonder you didn't develop ulcers, or at the very least indigestion, instead of just retreating to your head and getting depressed...
>
> You were passionate enough about your work at York House — but wore your body out because you didn't pay attention to *me*. Lots more excitement about work and study and projects — but where do you think your fatigue comes from? *Listen,* you dolt: you know enough, and your heart is OK, but you give yourself away to heal other people. Now that you know *in your head* that the cells in your body are alive and conscious and trying to take care of you, maybe you'll discover *me,* and remember that I serve that One, Life. Wake up !

We worked with the imagery of the *Vas* itself, the alchemical container in which the alchemist mixed his ingredients. It has many meanings, many names: the Philosophical Egg, the secret chamber, the womb, the lapis, the crucible... We struggled with the question: What do you trust absolutely? I wrote:

> I realize again that the inherent Nature of Things revealed by science is central to my faith. I am inspired by what John Hitchcock calls "the Wholeness Pattern". This is *in me,* in my body/mind, my psyche. And I do trust that God sustains my efforts to live in relation to this Pattern — that even when I make "mistakes" the Pattern will reassert itself in greater consciousness and renewed commitment.

The central imagery we worked with was the necessity for the *old* king (the Masculine) and the *old* queen (the Feminine) to die, and to be reborn. We struggled to verbalize our best understanding of the principles of Masculine and Feminine as embodied in the royal pair, and my journal reads:

> The question: What is the most valuable masculine principle that you follow, that directs your life? The most precious, the most golden, that you would not want to live without?
>
> Trust in the nature of Reality, Matter-Spirit, the Wholeness Pattern that is the Mystery at the heart of life...yet discernible in minute, concrete ways, gradually and continually revealing itself if I remain mindful and committed to cooperate with it. I am forever finding new ways to articulate this.
>
> Next question: What is the most cherished feminine principle that guides your life, that you could not live without? What does the Queen have that the King does not have?
>
> The words that come to me are gestation of new life, receptivity, power to nourish, intuitive wisdom, relatedness of the I to the Thou. Others spoke of Eros, birthing of the Self over and over, cherishing, that Love may fulfill itself.

And then, symbolically, we endured the descent of these cherished principles into dissolution in the Vas...revived them...and enacted their ritual marriage as the new sovereign principles. We spent many hours in this process, meditated, wrote, and shared.

On the last morning, having removed all the symbols from the center of the seminar room, we sat in silence, coming to terms with what we had experienced and "known" in new ways. And then, breaking the silence abruptly with an alchemical saying, John Petroni said: "Now go home. Burn all your books, lest you rend your heart in two." In the hush of that numinous silence you could almost hear the dismay. I felt the command profoundly, and knew that I had to come to terms with its necessity. "The will of God known in advance is not the will of God". My growing, my aging, must be lived in new ways, as yet unknown.

I came home, and over and over again had dreams of packing up to leave. And then came another reminder. Sylvia Ommanney had loaned me a book by a Poor Clare nun, Karen Karper, *Where God Begins to Be*[13], which was inspired by a statement from Meister Eckhart: "There where clinging to things ends, there God begins to be." She had left the security of her monastery after thirty years to go into retreat in a rugged area of the Appalachians, and one day in her tiny chapel, struggling to come to terms with the appalling difficulties of her new home, she "distinctly heard: 'You must lose all that you have become until now in order to become all that you really are.'"(p. 29) Reading that sentence, it was as if I had been struck in my solar plexus. Was this what the dreams were all about? Is this why I have been feeling more and more inward, more and more disquieted with outer activity, more and more exhausted?

I think it is what my aging is all about. At seventy I was not "old". At eighty, I was "beginning to feel old". At eighty-one, and especially in the last several months, I *am old*. Walking has become more difficult: my legs and back do not want to hold me up. The sense of vitality is slipping away. Describing the feeling to a friend, I heard myself say: "I feel as if I am collapsing into myself". Indeed, my body may be saying that I need to collapse into The Self...to let go. No more tasks, no more responding to demands made upon me, no more projects.

I truly feel that when this writing is completed, I will have "finished" a final major project. I will perhaps have completed what I need to do in this dimension of existence. And yet, to choose to let go, to be ready to die if indeed my work is finished, is still to "choose life, only that, and always, and at whatever risk..." For to die is to be re-born into another dimension of existence. Ann Ulanov writes:

> When the ego is related to the Self's point of view, and
> views things from the center of the whole, not just from
> its own one-sided partiality, it knows it will not die.[14]

I wrote the last paragraphs in present tense, in mid-April 1995. I was not choosing to *die*, only to let go into whatever my destiny might be. I was acutely aware that my body demanded attention, and when a way of renewal presented itself I responded almost instantly. A very old friend, Marguerite Davidson, had remarked one Sunday

---

[13]Karen Karper: *Where God Begins to Be*. Holland, Eerdman's, 1994.
[14]Ann Belfrod Ulanov: *The Wizard's Gate*. Switzerland, Daimon Verlag, 1994.

morning at church that she was "going back to Bavaria again this spring". Curious as to why she would go again, I asked what prompted her to return. Briefly she described a spa experience organized by a woman in West Vancouver, and told me where she had seen the ad. Something in me said *Yes!* and I phoned Giselle Roeder and in a leap of faith that this was what my psyche needed I borrowed the money to go.

Twelve seekers after health headed for Bad Woerishofen on April 17th, and spent three weeks in a third generation family kurpension where Anna and Karl Cebuli treated us to wonderful food, massage and water treatments developed by Sebastian Kneipp in the last century. I have never felt so looked after in my entire life! and slowly energy returned. The gardens of massed tulips and the incredibly beautiful meadows set against the background of the Alps nourished our souls. Marguerite and a new friend, Rose Gartner, and I spent an additional happy week in Lindau at the head of Lake Constance, once again generously looked after in a beautiful small hotel, the Hotel am Holdereggenpark, near the water and a short walk to the ancient island town. Boat trips and a bus tour to the Rhine Falls punctuated the walking and shopping on the old cobbled streets. We all knew that we would miss the landscape dotted with red roofs and church spires and fields of yellow canola seed, and in particular the special architecture of southern central Europe.

Home again, I turn once more with a different energy, to writing my story. What's more, I brought back some new ways of looking after an aging body: a massage mitt and strap for dry massage before a shower, and a habit of ending that shower with cold water — first the feet and legs, then the arms, the back and finally the front of me — something I thought I would never enjoy! I actually look forward to this morning routine following my usual exercises to strengthen back and shoulder muscles. One thing is very clear: it takes a lot more time to keep well when one is old! Walking is still exhausting, neglected muscles respond reluctantly, energies fluctuate. I've been a sedentary person, and am paying the price. And reluctantly — stubborn optimist that I am — I have had to acknowledge that *sometimes some* things can't be "fixed"!

In 1960, in response to a letter of congratulations on his 85th birthday, Jung wrote:

> Old age is only half as funny as one is inclined to think.
> It is at all events the gradual breaking down of the bodily

165

machine, with which foolishness identifies ourselves. It is indeed a major effort — the *magnum opus* in fact — to escape in time from the narrowness of its embrace and to liberate our mind to the vision of the immensity of the world, of which we form an infinitesimal part.[15]

My curiosity about how others experience aging has led to a search for autobiographies written in later years, and for books focusing on attitudes. Since I have been so fortunate in my mentors, and in my relationships with Jungians and Unitarians, I have been astonished by the amount of anger and resentment about the stereotypes impinging particularly upon women. In a feminist anthology by women, *Women and Aging*,[16] I found papers presented at a conference of the National Women's Studies Association in 1985. Barbara Macdonald addressed the fact that "the last thirty years of women's lives have been ignored in Women's Studies". I could hear her fury in the lines:

> From the beginning of this wave of the women's movement...the message has gone out to those of us over 60 that your "Sisterhood" does not include us, that those of you who are younger see us as men see us — that is, as women who used to be women but aren't any more. You do not see us in our present lives, you do not identify with our issues, you exploit us, you patronize us, you stereotype us. Mainly you ignore us.

Another paper in more moderate tone, by Shevey Healey, focuses on the issue of being ignored:

> It is difficult to hold on to one's own sense of self, one's own dignity when all around you there is no affirmation of you. At best there may be a patronizing acknowledgment; at worst, you simply do not exist.
> The oppressed old woman is required to be cheerful. But if you're smiling all the time, you acquiesce to being

---

[15]C.G.Jung: *Letters*, v.2, p.580.Princeton, N.J. Bollingen Series XCV:2., 1975.

[16]*Women and Aging*. Edited by Jo Alexander, Debi Berrow, Lisa Domitrovich, Margarita Donnelly and Cheryl McLean. Calyx Books, Corvallis, Oregon, 1986. See pages 20 and 61.

invisible and docile, participating in your own erasure. If you're not cheerful then you are accused of being bitter, mean, crabby, complaining ! A real Catch 22.

I was astonished, having experienced nothing of this in my own so-fortunate life space; and very sad to realize that these attitudes and conditions persist for many, many old women...and how much pain they cause.

While away in Bavaria I read one book in particular that offered a positive view and spoke to me in a number of ways about my own life, and about aging: *Older Than Time* by Allegra Taylor.[17] The author travelled the world in search of Women of Wisdom, and spent much time with honored elders, women who were pioneers and stalwarts of their communities. She cites Cara Caldwell Watson, a woman in New York State who at sixty-five finally realized her dream to be a theatre director, and quotes Cara as saying:

> I thought getting old was going to be so frightening. I thought life was like a wheel getting slower and slower but it isn't. Getting older in itself is no threat. You just get better, richer, more varied, more faceted. Life has fed you enough vital material that you feel full all the time. It is society's attitude that we need to change....Being old is not some kind of illness but a position of pride and respect that you have earned. People should want to be old. They should look forward to it.
>
> Life is like a garden; after you've blossomed in the spring and dropped your seeds in the summer, you remain for a while in the autumn and your colors are richer at that period of your flowering than at any other time. Being old brings so many advantages. It gives you a certain freedom to be eccentric. (p.27-8)

This is a woman speaking in her prime, her flowering. That was my experience too, as I entered Jungian training. But it is not everyone's good fortune to have the health and vitality to move forward vigorously in their late sixties and seventies. Debilitating illness can strike, and usher in an uninvited reorientation to suffering and dependency. That is feared more than death by most aging people.

---

[17]Allegra Taylor: *Older Than Time: A Grandmother's Search for Wisdom.* London, The Aquarian Press (an imprint of Harper/Collins), 1993.

On the other side of the world, in the Cook Islands, Allegra Taylor came to know another elder, Paddy, who had come very near to death with cancer.

> It was very humbling...the agony, the mess, the ter-
> ribleness, being totally dependent on other people. That
> whole experience had a great deal to do with my need to
> change and this gentle place makes it all possible. The
> simplicity and tranquillity of my life here gives me a sense
> of harmony and connectedness. Being connected both for-
> wards and backwards in time, both up and down to
> heaven and earth, and heart to heart to all other beings.
> As I see it, this is the only way to avoid the *fear* of aging. If
> you're growing outwards there's no room for fear because
> you're expanding into whatever comes next, you're wel-
> coming the change rather than trying to hang on to the
> past. (p.165)

If we are not so fortunate as to live in a tranquil place, or if we are struggling with poverty or discrimination, it must be very hard work indeed to achieve that kind of centered connectedness. If that were my lot, would I be able to create an inner place of tranquillity? I find it hard as it is ! And when the brain becomes dysfunctional with Alzheimer's disease, how mind and soul must suffer.

How thankful I am to be part of a church community where, if I have the energy, I can reach out to share the richness that Fate has granted. I have long wanted to do a church service on the signifi-cance of the man Jesus for Unitarians, which involves study of re-cent research to be integrated with my experience of the Records seminars. The 1990s have produced a wealth of new writing about the early Jesus movement and the documents of the Nag Hammadi collection of gospels. My excitement mounts as I read these books, thankful for eyes that can still see and relishing the challenge of new ideas. I am also able to do a little more work as a Jungian analyst, if I wish, and to participate in the training program of the North Pacific Institute for Analytical Psychology as a mentor. As the body wearies, mind and spirit are still blessedly free to explore. What the future holds, I hope to be able to accept. Once again, I remember that "the will of God known in advance is not the will of God." The challenge is to BE in the present moment.

And Now ...

Something else, too, came to me from my illness. I might formulate it as an affirmation of things as they are: an unconditional "yes" to that which is, without subjective protests—acceptance of the conditions of existence as I see them and understand them, acceptance of my own nature, as I happen to be ...[W]hen one follows the path of individuation, when one lives one's own life, one must take mistakes into the bargain; life would not be complete without them.

C.G. Jung[1]

The writing of my story has focused for the most part on experiences and ideas as they transformed my life. I have said that it was my intention to write my *spiritual* autobiography — in the sense that spirituality can be understood as "the essential temper of a person".[2] It is indeed a story more of my response to events and ideas than of the events and ideas in themselves.

---

[1]C.G.Jung: *Memories, Dreams, Reflections*. Pantheon Books, New York, 1961, p.297. The illness referred to was his near-fatal heart attack in 1944 at age sixty-nine. This would now be called a Near-Death experience, followed as it was by visions and a reluctance to return to mundane life.

[2]James W. Heisig: "The Mystique of the Nonrational", p.171 in David Ray Griffin, Ed.: *Archetypal Process: Self and Divine in Whitehead, Jung, and Hillman*. Evanston, Illinois, Northwestern University Press, 1989.

Although I am a Jungian analyst, I have not wanted, for instance, to discuss Jungian theory, even though there are many interesting shifts in current approaches. In particular there are significant changes around issues of the feminine principle — for example, in Claire Douglas' fine review entitled *The Woman in the Mirror*[3] and Demaris Wehr, *Jung and Feminism*[4]. The "post-Jungian" world has at last matured in our attitude to Jung himself, recognizing that he was very much a man of his times as well as a pioneer, and a human being as well as a man of great wisdom. In the wake of the 1995 International Congress of Jungian analysts in Zurich, a perceptive participant, Richard Corelli, wrote:

> Dr. Samuels [of London] spoke of our not having mourned Jung completely. Someone in the audience insightfully commented that we were coming together at this congress to hold a Requiem for Jung. It seemed to me as if the baton was being passed from one generation to the next and that there was a subtle or not so subtle transformation occurring in the Jungian world. We are no longer Jungian analysts but are now analytical psychologists. It is time to loosen the personal identification with Jung as a person and organize our identity more around our function and relationship to the unconscious.[5]

This seems to me a very accurate perception.

One of the great gifts of working as a Jungian analyst is the satisfaction of "presence", the being-with another searching soul in a slow-paced, concentrated listening, intuiting, mutual exploration. I have only briefly worked with one client "on the couch"; my preferred mode has always been face to face where eye contact discourages evasion. In this manner I've been privileged to know in incredible depth some very remarkable human beings, and been challenged in my own being-ness to live that of which I speak. It is a

---

[3]Claire Douglas: *The Woman in the Mirror: Analytical Psychology and the Feminine*. Boston, Sigo Press, 1990.

[4]Demaris Wehr: *Jung and Feminism: Liberating Archetypes*. Boston, Beacon Press, 1987.

[5]Richard J. Corelli, M.D.: "Jung's Requiem", p. 5, in an occasional in-house publication of the C.G.Jung Institute of San Francisco, *Connected Works*. Used with permission.

process that *demands* continuous learning and tracking of dreams and self-reflection. It is also an occupation which increases in riches as one ages. I forget my aching body as I sit quietly, focused and alert to the struggling, growing consciousness of my client.

The importance of the seminars on the Records of the life of Jesus I have already discussed. The challenges of career changes have been enormous. But it is the *impact* of all of this that is now resonating within me, in this liminal space of "old age."

I realize there have been many omissions, both of relationships, and of day-to-day life and the details which give me pleasure. Some of the omissions are intentional, out of respect for the privacy of important persons still living. This is particularly true of love relationships...the joyous, sometimes mystical experiences of lovemaking which have been such a gift in the decade of my seventies. There were long periods after Fred's death when the longing for a partner was almost overwhelming. I recall kneeling before the figure of Kuan Yin, crying, praying that "if it be the will of God, grant me a companion". And needing always to add: "Nevertheless, Thy will be done." Like many women in their later years, I recognize that such a partner would need to be equally committed to the path of individuation, to open communication, to the freedom to be *real* with each other. When one has lived a long time alone there would need also to be space in our home for being together and *not - to-* gether. Today, living a more inward life, that longing has subsided, even though companionship and mutual support in aging are a deep desire. And even though reading biographies of truly great and lasting love evoke sadness that my experiences of deep intimacy have been for me but moments in time. Laura Huxley's biography of her brief but beautiful marriage with Aldous is entitled *This Timeless Moment*[6] and however brief the gift of love, it is indeed *timeless*.

One such love I want to acknowledge because it has evolved and transcended what was in the beginning a primarily sexual relationship, and today we enjoy a richly honest friendship. In the thesis I wrote for my Jungian training, I had described the depth of connection with Evan (not his real name) as "The beginning of love in relation to the Self." It is because of that grounding that we have been able to weather many mutual hurts and each time move beyond the

---

[6]Laura Archera Huxley: *This Timeless Moment: A Personal View of Aldous Huxley*. New York, Farrar, Straus & Giroux, 1968.

break. We are agreed that it is because we are both committed to "growing" as persons into an increasingly responsive and spiritual life, that our quiet love endures. Our lives have much in common, and as "retired" people we both love to read and write, and Evan continues at times his teaching in an academic setting. We both appreciate our independence, and are grateful for our separate homes, enough income to enjoy good things, and reasonably good health despite limitations.

One great regret will remain with me: that the sense of "family" — mothering and grandmothering — has always been sidelined to the compelling urgency of individual growth and work in the world. There must have been in me a deep yearning for a lively family life. Else why would I have been so moved by stories like "Room for One More" where a couple adopts children of many racial backgrounds who need a home? And families whose members gather around the piano to make music?...It's true that work for me was a financial necessity; for many reasons Morgan had not helped us in that way. But the urgency to do what I felt to be creative work is the inescapable "me" of which Jung wrote; a fact of my life. It was highlighted when reading Allegra Taylor's book, *Older Than Time,* as she described her homesickness for family as she travelled the world. I don't remember *ever* being homesick even when I grew weary of travel. This does not mean that my sons and their families are not important to me, and a source of deep satisfaction as their lives develop. I have written little about them, sometimes out of respect for privacy, sometimes because geographical distance has limited contact.

I've written a little about Reed and Frank in their earlier years; I'd like to bring their stories up to date. Both studied Mathematics, and both taught for a time in Mexico, but then their paths diverged. Frank did his doctoral program in Canberra, Australia, took a government job in Saskatchewan, and is now teaching at Capilano College in North Vancouver and enjoying it. His office at home is packed with computer equipment (he tutors me on occasion), and his home with skis, ice skates, roller blades and outdoor paraphernalia, gathered as he learned to keep up with his athletic son and to share his small daughter's activities. His second wife, Sheila, is a delightfully creative person, both in arts and crafts, as an enthusiastic mother, and in working with people. Both of them have helped me enormously in the practical tasks of moving and installing shelving and hanging paintings. I feel totally supported, and appreciative of their caring.

My first grand-daughter, Katryn, was born in Australia when her parents were study-ing there and I was at U.C.L.A. Today, fully bi-lingual, she is complet-ing her third year as a volunteer at L'Arche north of Paris, the first com-munity founded by Jean Vanier for handicapped people. Her brother Kevin graduated from high school with honors, won a handsome scholarship to the University of Brit-ish Columbia and has completed his first year. Athlete that he is, he is planning to train in Sports Medicine. The third grandchild in my Van-couver family is Megan, a lively nine-year-old following in the bilin-gual footsteps of her step-siblings, and danc-ing her way through her young life. She is the only one of my grand-children born here in Vancouver, and one of my favorite snapshots is of a joyous Me holding her in my arms when only a few hours old.

I've not been so fortu-nate in knowing well my California family, although

Frank Harris, 1989

*Reed Harris representing his
computer firm at a conference*

we try to visit from time to time. Reed and Karen chose to live on Maui for the first five years, and I went to their wedding, and later to visit one Christmas after their second child was born. Reed shares his brother's interest in computers, but not in teaching, and for a long time earned a precarious living as a highly skilled carpenter. Jobs on Maui were scarce, and they moved to California, just as opportunities diminished. He is very much an artist, and I've always wished he would have the leisure to continue with sculpture and stained glass, but these years have been difficult. Now, after intensive training and securing a job in computer programming, he is at last working at something he really enjoys. Karen has been a marvellous support through poverty and depression, anchored as she is in a spiritual approach to life. Her own great joy is as a mother, and she teaches the children at home and is active in the Home School Association. She is also very knowledgeable about healthy foods, with a large

Karen and Reed Harris,1985

Family Gathering, July 30, 1987
Megan, Sheila, Clare, Reed, Karen
Kevin, Frank, Michael

175

vegetable garden, and Michael and Willow sparkle with energy. Both children love swimming and gymnastics.

As they grew to manhood, both sons took initiative to know their father better, having lived so far from him for so many years. In his later years Morgan enjoyed teaching night classes in writing and many of his students joined him for parties at his home. He had re-married shortly after our divorce, and they had built a house which he designed, but the marriage had not been satisfying for either partner, and he lived alone. Frank made it possible for Morgan to come to Vancouver for a number of Christmas celebrations, so he knew these grandchildren; and he also visited Maui, where his older sister Elizabeth lived as well as Reed's family. In his last years, after a severe stroke and hospitalization, Reed and Frank both spent time with him in Los Angeles. It was then that a family "secret" came to light. I had known that Morgan had had a teen-age marriage which had been annulled, and that there was a child born of that union, but during our marriage Morgan never spoke of this, nor did he have contact with that son, and I completely forgot about it. What none of us knew was that Morgan had finally connected with Jack and they had become close. The fact that there were now *three* sons involved in decision-making led to conflict. Morgan was helpless, dependent on technology to continue living, and at one critical point the doctor asked whether life should be artificially sustained. There was strong disagreement over what to do, Jack in particular wanting to believe that his father would one day recover. The result was that Morgan lingered for a year and a half, able to understand, but unable to move or speak, and on a respirator. Perhaps he himself didn't want to let go of life. One never knows. He had left no instructions, not even a will.

* * * * *

Responding to a continuing hunger for glimpses of other lives as perceived in old age, I have — like a detective — followed clues to other autobiographies published by anyone writing in their later years. Recently I came upon *Leaves of the Tulip Tree*[7] by Juliette

---

[7]Juliette Huxley: *Leaves of the Tulip Tree*. London, John Murray (Publishers) Ltd., 1986.

Huxley, the wife of Julian Huxley, and have been fascinated by the picture she paints of the Bloomsbury group in the London of the first World War. I have also experienced the old nagging feeling of wishing I were "more like" someone else. Her brilliant word-paintings of personalities and relationships in another world are of a different order from my capabilities. I have been grateful for Jung's reminder of accepting the uniqueness of being oneself.

A statement she makes on the eve of her fateful marriage struck a responsive chord:

> No one's life, in this world, is an open document — neither to others, nor to ourselves. Our private memories black out essential links, which we seek for in vain, in a kind of despair.[8]

I have wrestled with the "private memories" of life with Morgan, spending a sleepless night writing and re-writing in imagination the years of our growing estrangement. How much openness is wise or appropriate? How much would be of interest to anyone reading the story? In the end, many of those scenes seem essentially private, and I have respected that.

Life as I live it today feels more urgent, and that is the picture I want to share as the writing draws to a close. What, for instance are the daily pleasures of someone who has been so active until recently, and now has limited energy?

My live-in companions are my two cats! Yorkie must now be about twelve years old, an Old Queen with an expressive face who, although refusing to sit on my lap, communicates affection by rubbing noses. When I acquired her about six years ago she was so sedentary that I bought a Siamese kitten to entice her into playfulness, and she quickly responded to his eight-week-old need for mothering. The two of them sleep together, and engage in mutual licking that is a delight to watch. Tomo, named for Tomo Geshe Rinpoche, Lama Govinda's teacher, is utterly beautiful as he lies on top of me while resting. I recall once exclaiming aloud, "How did God ever make anything so beautiful!" But true to the opposites of life, he has fangs; and as well as being affectionate and playful, he is jealous and almost daily picks a fight with Yorkie, usually to get my attention. He

---

[8]Juliette Huxley: *Leaves of the Tulip Tree*. London, John Murray (Publishers) Ltd., 1986.

chews all my plants, poisonous and otherwise, gobbles his food, and then ejects it on the carpet. But I love him...I love them both. The cats are a great expense when I want to be away, but such good company and wonderful to come home to. Friends who have heard me bemoan the fact that I've never learned to play will appreciate their influence! That lack of playfulness in my nature is one of the factors in my difficulties in being the kind of grandmother I would like to be.

My companions are also the peoples of the world, brought alive for me by bulletins from the non-governmental organizations doing the work I cannot do...supporting the efforts of ordinary people everywhere to sustain hope in a tragically difficult world through projects that create a better life. Their stories come to life in the pages of the Inter Pares newsletter[9] and *The New Internationalist*[10] and a dozen others, including some closer to home. Over the years this kind of reading has given me a sense of being a planetary citizen, while the reading in quantum physics has led to experiencing a belonging in the universe. Even as an introverted elder, living alone, I am aware that I am not alone. This does not preclude moments of *feeling* alone; then I need to remind myself that my inner and outer life are richly peopled.

Daily I realize how important, how *essential*, beauty is in my life. When searching through my teen-age collection of poems, I came upon one by Robert Bridges[11] with the marginal notation: *this was my motto as I left for Branksome Hall.*

> I love all beauteous things,
>   I seek and adore them;
> God hath no better praise,
> And man in his hasty days
> Is honored for them.
>
> I too will something make
>   And joy in the making;
> Altho' tomorrow it seem
> Like the empty words of a dream
>   Remembered on waking.

---

[9]Inter Pares: 58 Arthur Street, Ottawa, Ontario, Canada K1R 7B9.

[10]*The New Internationalist*. 35 Riviera Drive, Markham, Ontario, Canada L3R 8N4.

[11]Robert Bridges, 1844-1930: "I Love All Beauteous Things", in a 1930's high school text, *A Selection of English Poetry*. Long out of print.

Often and often I have found myself repeating these lines...although now I omit the last two, aware that the words of a dream are anything but "empty". Many aspects of beauty arrest my attention...the quality of light in the sky, the shape of a tree, the symmetry of a Canada goose or the spring family of Mallard ducklings in the lagoon where I live. In my present condominium where I face the water, the city, and the mountains, I awake each morning to an expanse of sky that reminds me of Tony Onley's paintings of northern clouds in soft grays, surely a gift at dawn. Some of my happiest memories are of landscapes, like the pine-dotted golden hills of California, so reminiscent of a similar scene from the ranch in the Okanagan. Today this cluster of memories includes the undulating greens of Bavaria with the always-red roofs and onion spires and the snow-covered Alps in the background.

Another type of beauty is equally captivating — the infinite colors and patterns of fabrics, and the design and texture of beautiful clothes. When I worked in Bill Beckett's architectural office in California, my taste in house design and furnishings was nurtured by the array of magazines available to me, publications from France and Italy as well as America. I'm sure my mother's sense of beauty and color shaped my responses; she did everything with an eye for order and harmony. Equally, I love native crafts and jewelry, a love well satisfied in my month in Peru, and in a holiday with Reed in Mexico one Christmas when he was teaching math at the American School in Mexico City.

Everywhere I turn in my small home there are paintings and artifacts that enrich my days. Many are prints but a few are originals, each with special meaning. Over my bed hangs a painting in acrylic and silk by Pat MacBain entitled "Dawn of a Holy Day", and as I turn my head on awakening, a charcoal drawing of "Woman in the Moon" by Elizabeth Nell — a gift from my daughter-in-law, Sheila McFadzean to celebrate the awakening of the Feminine during my Jungian training. Over the counter between kitchen and dining area, catching the light from two directions, is a stained glass panel, a creation of Reed's which I treasure. From the dining table I enjoy a painting of elephants on silk from India, a gift from Frank and Katryn when they travelled there together. Two with treasured memories are the work of Clement Wilenchek, a friend and lover from California days — a painting of two spirited young horses, which he gave me one birthday, and a Head of Christ which came to him as a vision during meditation... Some are pastels from my own "active imagination". Some are gift cards which evoke a sense of Spirit. A weaving of the gods of Navajo sand-paintings warms the wall behind the couch. A recent acquisition is a limited edition print by the Salish artist, Susan Point, entitled "Pacific Spirit" — a work that made my heart beat with excitement as I watched it being wrapped. All bring joy to eye and heart.

I want in particular to speak of two small paintings by Sylvia Ommanney: one an abstract of the Navajo goddess, Changing Woman; one of oleander by the swimming pool at Four Springs. These speak of shared experiences with a very special friend whose generous spirit contributes so much to my life, week by week. We try to breakfast together each Saturday, talking of our pressing concerns and loves and hopes. Sylvia is a tall, beautiful woman in her fifties with a remarkable gift for friendship with innumerable people of all ages. Her artistry includes painting, needlework and liturgical arts. Her talents range from cooking to worship services to business acumen to mediation in conflicted situations. And her adoring husband, Tudor, much her senior, recovered from a serious heart condition ten years ago to vigorous health in the warmth of their mutual love. The age difference, and a now recurring angina, mean that they face a future of certain loss; but they talk about it, and manage to live in the present, rejoicing in the world of nature, the spiritual community of their church, and friends. They are an inspiration to all of us.

A passage in Laura Huxley's book captures all these experiences. The scene is the hospital room where Aldous is dying, full of equipment,

his favorite roses...the only deliverance:

Now Aldous could not see more than two feet away. That morning I arranged the slant of his pillows and the spotlight behind them. Then I kept a rose very close to him, just where he could see it, feel it, without moving. First, I turned the rose slowly so he could see it from different angles. He looked at it for a while with the magnifying glass, then he let go of it and relaxed his hands. He lay in complete comfort with the rose two inches away from his face, breathing it. Salmon pink, perfectly harmonious, luminously alive, the rose was looking at Aldous and

Aldous was looking at the rose. There was perfect communication between the two — and complete silence. As
Aldous opened himself to the rose his face became peaceful and smooth. Time stopped. We were motionless for a
long while. Then I asked, "Is it enough?"

Almost inaudibly, but with the utmost clarity, he answered, "It is never enough. Never enough." It was the
faintest whisper, but it had the intensity of a thousand
voices. They were saying, "Never enough of beauty.
Never enough of love. Never enough of life...."[12]

Reading *Archetypal Process: Self and Divine in Whitehead, Jung,
and Hillman* which my friends Marli and Gunter Schmidt-Weinmar
brought to my attention, I was delighted to find in one of the papers
a statement by James Hillman that this experience of beauty

refers to the gasp, the 'aha', the 'uh' of the breath of
wonder. It is recognition of the 'eachness' of things,
or...like the Eastern notion of *suchness* .[13]

The experience is linked to aesthetics and to Whitehead's intuition of God as "the poet of the world", as "the Eros of the universe".
(p. 111)

Of still greater inspiration is the Navajo conception of Beauty. I
have always felt a closer kinship with their mythology than with that
of the Greeks, and recently I came upon a statement that "speaks to
my condition", as the Quakers say. Peter Gold translates a phrase
from a Navajo sacred incantation as: "journeying into old age by way
of spiritual beauty". This, he says, refers to

the process of constant spiritual renewal leading to a
ripe old age (the mark of a consummated spiritual life).[14]

Always there is music. Daily I bless the Canadian Broadcasting
Corporation network for their classical programs, and pray that our
treasured CBC system will be able to withstand the onslaught of gov-

---

[12]Laura Archera Huxley: *op.cit.*, p.66-7.

[13]Stanley R. Hopper: "Once more: the Cavern beneath the Cave", in
David Ray Griffin: *Archetypal Process: Self and Divine in Whitehead, Jung,
and Hillman*, Ch.5, p.123.

[14]Peter Gold: *Navajo and Tibetan Sacred Wisdom: The Circle of the Spirit.*
Rochester, Vermont, Inner Traditions, 1984.

ernment cuts and multinational corporate values. Years ago I bought good tape recording equipment, and Frank and Sheila, for my eightieth birthday, gave me a teak cabinet to house the hundreds of cassette tapes and C.D.'s. The members of the Jung Intensive Study Group 2, knowing of this love, recently gave me a gift certificate to purchase recordings at The Magic Flute. And I gave myself the luxury of membership in a Canadian firm offering a rich array of music at discount, and almost each month indulge my pleasure. This will be increasingly important as my eyesight limits reading and my back tires from walking.

That I cannot count on continuing good eyesight was brought home to me vividly in December, 1995, when one of those sudden deficits of old age made its appearance. At breakfast with Sylvia I was unable to read the pencilled notes she wanted to share; and at the symphony concert that night with Evan I couldn't read the program notes. Thanks to Sylvia's connections with a gifted eye specialist, my doctor obtained an emergency appointment three days later. Sylvia's "blue Volvo transport" took me to his office, and after four hours of testing the verdict came: some vascular leak in my one good eye (promptly stopped with laser treatment) plus increased cataract development in that eye, and — which is more serious — some macular degeneration of the retina. "But you will probably have five or six good years yet if I remove the cataract."

I came home relieved, but remembering Marie Gerhardt-Olly whose blindness stemmed from macular degeneration. Exhausted, I fell into a deep sleep and dreamed of Alan Cashmore, experiencing once again the depth of our love. Awake, I was aware that had our life circumstances been different we might have been lovers, perhaps partners. Maybe the dream says, *Remember what riches are yours, even as you contemplate loss*. The healing quality of that encounter lingered throughout the day.

This past summer I decided to take singing lessons! Most of my life I've thought I couldn't follow a tune, and scarcely opened my mouth even to sing well-known favorites. Was this part of the Silence in my childhood home, the fear of speaking out? For a time when the boys were little, Morgan and another couple and I took singing lessons and I learned that I *could* sing if I allowed myself to follow the piano...but I lost that confidence when the stress increased. So now I wanted to be able to chant in meditation, and to sing hymns where words and music were inspiring, and simple songs. I found a wonderful teacher, Judy Maas, only a few years younger than I; and bought an electronic keyboard so that I could have notes to follow. The old fear was constricting at first, and some days when my vitality is at low ebb, the resonance fades. But I am finding my voice! And loving the experience.

Whatever the physical limitations, I *can* still read, still explore new realms of knowledge. Marli and Gunter keep discovering books that connect quantum physics and psychology and process theology, and generously send me photocopied excerpts which entice me to keep ordering books, both from the library and from my favorite bookstore. They introduced me to Burton Mack's *The Lost Gospel: The Book of Q and Christian Origins*[15] which started my pursuit of the historical Jesus, the man behind the Christian myth of the dying and resurrecting god. In combination with the published work of the Jesus Seminars, and the Gospel of Thomas uncovered in 1945 as part of the Nag Hammadi library, I begin to have a more lively sense of the Palestine Jesus lived in, and of the teachings the gospel writers drew upon. Following the threads from book to book, like Ariadne in the labyrinth, I prepared the December 1995 church service on Jesus which I had offered to present.

The process summoned new energies. The desire to *learn* never fades, even with an often aching body. And the sense of connectedness with loved friends, old and new, blesses me constantly.

What more could I ask of life? As the *Gospel of Thomas* records Jesus as saying "If you bring forth what is within you, what you bring forth will save you"...and bring you joy. What is deep within all of us is the image of God; and I am eternally grateful both for the teachings of Jesus as I came to understand them at Four Springs, and for the work of Jung that has permeated my life — both of these over a span of fifty years.

Jung was driven to discover the myth of his own life; and I have often tried to find words to express what my own might be. Perhaps in writing my story as a *spiritual* autobiography I have indirectly answered that question. Jung wrote in his own autobiography, *Memories, Dreams, Reflections* (p.340), that

> The need for mythic statements is satisfied when we
> frame a view of the world which adequately explains the

---

[15] Burton L. Mack: *The Lost Gospel: The Book of Q and Christian Origins.* Harper San Francisco, 1993.

meaning of psychic wholeness, from the co-operation between conscious and unconscious.[16]

I hope my sense of what is involved in that cooperation has in
some way been said. For me, the very writing itself has been satisfying beyond all expectation. Questions and feedback from early versions, and now from my discerning editor, Diana Douglas, have
forced me to look deeply at every phase of my life.

I had done that during the Jungian training, and realized that I
had left behind the negatives associated with the pattern of the
father's daughter. I felt I had touched the mystery of the Great
Mother, and had indeed reclaimed and experienced my feminine
Self. The acknowledgement conveyed by the Women of Distinction
award affirmed my work in the world as mentor and educator. Working with Ladson Hinton and my Jungian colleagues had given me a
further sense of creative teamwork in a beloved group.

What the writing accomplished has been beyond those realiza-
tions. In some mysterious way I have gained a more solid sense of
who I really *am*...of the "true nature" which is living through this
moment in time...of the soul that moves through eternal Time. This
is the myth of my own *always becoming*.

---

[16]C.G.Jung: *Memories, Dreams, Reflections*. New York, Pantheon Books,
1961.

EPILOGUE

> Creation is a profound ongoing experience...an evolving force. To serve the element of becoming is the meaning in our lives.
>
> Laurens van der Post

ALWAYS BECOMING. Indeed, the challenge is always there: *Choose Life, only that, and always.*

Six months after writing the last chapter the aging process has catapulted me into a new process revolving around failing vision. In "Body and Soul" I gave thanks for eyes that could still see. Now I must come to terms with the need for a magnifying glass to read, and with the increased fatigue.

Cataract surgery on my one good eye took place at the end of February 1996...a marvel of new technology. Dr. Finlay predicted "greatly improved vision", and then added: "But I'm sorry I can't promise how long it will last. We simply cannot predict how fast macular degeneration of the retina will develop...sometimes slowly, sometimes quickly." Three times during the recovery period he spoke of this, and I heard the warning.

The seven misty weeks without glasses were a foretaste of what degeneration might be like — no reading whatever, no driving, difficulty in seeing the destination names on the buses until they were beside me, asking clerks for help in buying groceries. Key telephone numbers were converted to large bold black. Ladson Hinton faxed me letters about the Jungian training program in size 18 bold type. Cam Trowsdale offered to read to me, brought tapes, repaired my tape recorder. I re-discovered my small collection of taped lectures, including an inspiring one by Laurens van der Post on the crisis of meaning. I discovered taped books at the libary. Music was a truly heavenly resource...But it wasn't easy. My journal of April 8 records:

> I'm very aware that if diminished vision is part of my fate, I may not go so gently into that good night. At times in these six weeks I have felt slightly depressed, which is an avoidance of the feelings of grief and foreboding. It will take work to remain centered and in touch with those feelings. I live alone, and could easily become isolated. *Everything* is an effort, even caring for my cats.

When I got my prescription for new glasses, Dr. Finlay seemed pleased.

"Your vision is 20/40, and that means driving is still legal." But when I put on those new glasses the blur was a shock, and while some of the blur was remedied by a change in the second lens, driving doesn't feel safe. Although my distance vision may still improve slightly, I will probably sell my car at the end of the summer. The failure of the predicted improvement felt like a disaster. Since most of my friends have benefited so greatly from cataract surgery, I can only conclude that the macular degeneration is progressing.

Gradually, I found myself thinking about a retirement residence ...no more housekeeping. On May 28th I requested space in Arbutus Manor, a quiet place with beautiful gardens and with people and activities when I feel like joining in. I will have time for reflection, the leisure to read (with that magnifying glass) and ponder what I read, and my faithful computer for writing. I hope to enter in the early fall. The summer willl find me sorting, giving away, selling my condominium. Thank goodness I have that asset to help me finance the cost of living in such a lovely space.

My morning meditation that week found me facing some of the feelings.

I will find it hard to destroy my files and their many stories of people and projects. Dismantling my library feels, in some strange way, like dismantling a part of my identity! But *sharing* those valuables will be satisfying as well. A more difficult task will be designating treasures like my mother's silver and beloved objects to family members with caring and fairness. The summer's work will not be easy...I will need to allow for grieving.

Concern for my cats was a matter of more than personal loss: *their* well-being matters greatly. I sent out a prayer to the Universe that there would be a loving home for them. Then, at the last supper gathering of the Jung Study Group I shared my plan of moving to Arbutus Manor, and was searching for a home for Yorkie and Tomo. Immediately, Shiella Fodchuk asked, "Would you let us have them? We love cats, and there's lots of room. Solomon [their cat] will get used to company...I've always loved your cats. I've even wanted to ask you, if anything should happen to you, could we please have Yorkie and Tomo?" My delight amounted almost to disbelief: could this be true? Hours before, I had prepared an ad for the little local paper, having missed an earlier deadline by a day. Now, plans are made: Shiella will bring her husband to meet my cats, and they will move to their new home in August, when Shiella has her holidays. The Universe heard my prayer!

Two events have helped to shift the focus from "giving up" toward a sense of something holding new possibilities. While waiting for an appointment one day, I found myself visualizing how it might be for me in a retirement community. I don't find casual conversation easy. How will I connect with people with whom I may have little in common? Suddenly an idea came: I can always invite a person to "tell me your story". My whole feeling changed! Instead of just "retiring to a restful place", it *could* be an adventure! *Everyone's* story is interesting to me, and I love to listen.

Then, one evening, reading in my favorite journal, the *Noetic Sciences Review*, I came upon the title: "The Unplanned Organization: Learning from Nature's Emergent Creativity".[1] It reminded me of *Always Becoming*. Margaret Wheatley says some important things succinctly:

> Life is capable of creating patterns and structures and organizations all the time, without conscious rational direction, planning, or control. (p.17)
>
> In a self-organizing world, we see change as a power, a presence, a capacity, that is available. It's part of the way the world works — a spontaneous movement toward new forms of order, new patterns of creativity.

---

[1] Margaret Wheatley: *Noetic Sciences Review.* Spring 1996, p.16.

...life wants to happen as a community and we are all part of it. (p.18)

We live in a world which is constantly exploring what's possible, finding new combinations — not struggling to survive, but playing, tinkering, to find what's possible. (p.19)

A memory, April 1977, at the Unitarian Chruch. I am speaking at the Thursday evening service on the topic: "Allowing Myself to Happen". *Unplanned!* Yes indeed. The idea has always haunted me, ever since I heard about a workshop of that title from my friend Pat Baker. But when it came to writing that sermon I *could not* put pen to paper until the day of the service, and only then because of a dream the night before. Someone asked me: "How could you risk that?" And my answer was something like Margaret Wheatley's statements about the inherent nature of life of which I have a "felt sense", an intuitive knowing. I have learned to *trust* that Life supports the efforts of those who choose to cooperate with the thrust toward Wholeness. Einstein is said to have remarked that the most important question each of us answers for ourselves is: "Is the universe friendly or not?" Liz Greene's concept of Fate says, *Yes.*

A last journal entry, May 26, 1996, titled: "The Dawn of a Holy Day":

> I had spent a lovely evening, listening to Venetian Vespers, and reading the Spring issue of "Noetic Sciences Review" with its glorious cover painting of golden tulips by Alan Paulson. I ordered a book by the Russian psychiatrist, Olga Kharitidi, *Entering the Circle.*[2] Even though my vision is deteriorating want to meditate on books like this which speak of spiritual awakening. It was a peaceful evening, with the quality of time that I hope to experience at Arbutus Manor.
>
> I awoke at dawn with a dream:
>
> *I am watching a young mother with her year-old son who is exploring the courtyard and talking about what he finds. He has extraordinary eyes: large, knowing, pale turquoise*

---

[2]Olga Kharitidi: *Entering the Circle: A Russian Psychiatrist's Journey into Siberian Shamanism.* San Francisco. An Institute of Noetic Sciences Book (with Gloria Press, Inc.), 1995.

like a clear mountain lake. His gaze as he looks at me is direct. I think: she is mothering this child well...

Later, it is morning and the household is asleep. I go outside, and in the company of an unknown person behind me, begin climbing a nearby mountain. We've not been here before and are surprised at the terrain. It is stone, smooth, honey-colored, and wrinkled like the hide of the Skeleton Coast elephant I saw on television last night.

It will be a steep climb, and I decide to return for some food. It is now ten o'clock, but no-one is around. I notice a window open and realize my father must be up and about somewhere. I get a bagel and cream cheese and plan to return to the mountain, longing to be there with the wind and the clouds. They will find me there later, peaceful, and know that I have rejoined the elements.

What a beautiful prospect...to return to the Source...to remember.

Glossary of Jungian Terms

Active Imagination. A process of conscious interaction between the ego and an image or symbol from the unconscious, through writing, drawing, sculpture, etc.

Anima. The unconscious feminine component of a man's psyche, personified in dreams by a female figure and usually projected onto a woman in the outer world. In homosexual relationships, it is the archetypal feminine projected onto a person of the same sex. It is related to soul, eros.

Animus. The unconscious masculine component of a woman's personality, personified in dreams by a male figure and usually projected onto a man in the outer world. In homosexual relationships, it lis the archetypal masculine projected onto a person of the same sex. It is related to spirit, initiative.

Archetype. A universal pattern from the collective unconscious which appears to consciousness as image or motif, as in myth, fairy tale, religion. Examples: the Wise Old Man or Woman, the Divine Child, the Witch, the Father/Mother.

Complex. An emotionally charged image or idea rooted in personal experience but unconscious until recognized, operating irrationally. At its core is an archetype.

Ego. The center of consciousness, experienced as "I", and having the responsibility for conscious decision and choice, and for relating to the Self. (See below)

Feeling. One of the four psychic functions in Jungian typology, which evaluates experience. Not to be confused with emotion, which is irrational affect prompted by a complex. (See above)

Individuation. The conscious choosing by the ego to relate to the Self, resulting in increasing psychic wholeness.

Inflation. A psychological state of over-valuing one's self-image, or identifying with the ideal or pseudo-self. Negative inflation is an unrealistic under-valuing of one's personality.

Intuition. One of the four psychic functions. It sees possibilities, recognized "hunches", has flashes of insight, experiences and trusts inner knowing.

Persona. The role played by the conscious ego; or unconscious identification with the self-image, often to the point of hiding the true personality.

Self. The archetype of wholeness and the center of the psyche, experienced in dream symbols such as the pearl of great price, the butterfly, etc. Jung saw the Self (usually spelled with capital S) as the divine imago, the image of God within the human psyche.

Shadow. The traits or attitudes repressed or rejected or ignored by the conscious ego, operating out of awareness but visible to others.

Symbol. "The best possible expression for something essentially unknown. Symbolic thinking is non-linear, right-brain oriented; it is complementary to logical, linear, left-brain thinking."[1]

Thinking. In Jungian typology, one of the four psychic functions, characterized by discrimination and rationality, having a preference for logical, linear, left-brain functioning in evaluating experience.

Transcendent Function. The reconciling "third" which emerges from the unconscious after the conflicting opposites have been consciously differentiated, and the tension between them held.

---

[1] Joan Dexter Blackmer: *Acrobats of the Gods: Dance and Transformation.* Toronto, Inner City Books, 1989, p.115.

ORDER FORM

Always Becoming: An Autobiography

_____Copies @ $19.95 (Can)ea. _____
_____Copies @ $17.95 (US) ea._____
$5.00 for 1 book, add $2.00 for each additional book for Shipping & Handling _____
Total enclosed_____

Make cheque or money order payable to:
Clare M. Buckland

for VISA and Mastercard
circle appropriate card
fill in card number and expiration date.

☐☐☐☐☐☐☐☐☐☐☐☐☐

Expiration date:_____

Signature:_____

Ship To:
Name_____
Address_____
City, Province/State_____
Postal/Zip Code_____
Phone_____(work)_____(home)

PEANUT BUTTER PUBLISHING
Suite 230 - 1333 Johnston Street
Pier 32, Granville Island, Vancouver, B.C., V6H 3R9
For more information call 604-688-0320
WWW home page: http://www.pbppublishing.com
e-mail: pnutpub@aol.com

Thank you for your order!